Congratulations! You have just taken the first step toward the successful pursuit of your personal fortune. The information you hold in your hand will provide you with an easy-to-understand, fundamental knowledge about successful investing. You no longer have to be on the outside looking in. You have taken the first step into the world of money.

You will find the world of money to be a place with rhyme and reason and *not* the enormously complicated place it may look like from the outside. There are only two ways to Make Money Make Money—you can use it to *own* or to *loan*. And there are only three basic tools you will use—stocks, bonds, and banks. All possible investments will boil down to these three money tools. The trick is to know when to use which tool—and that is what this book is all about! It will show you what the tools of the world of money were designed to do and then will give you a step-by-step guide for your *own* personal wealth building program!

GOOD LUCK ON YOUR NEW ADVENTURE!

D0956814

MAKE MONEY MAKE MONEY

A SIMPLE GUIDE TO INVESTING

MAKE MONEY MAKE MONEY

A SIMPLE GUIDE TO INVESTING

By Roger A. Wynkoop

Published By:
Success Now, Inc.
P.O. Box 32530
Tucson, AZ 85751

Published by arrangement with Success Now, Inc.
Copyright © 1983 by Roger A. Wynkoop

First Edition
Library of Congress Catalog Card Number 83-060735
ISBN 0-912545-00-3
Printed in the United States of America
    84 85 86 87 10 9 8 7 6 5 4 3

To my wife, Diane, whose support and assistance made this work possible.

CONTENTS

CHARTS AND TABLES

Introduction

At last, here is a book that will provide you with all the basic information necessary for intelligent investing. It is written in easy-to-read and understandable *layman's language*. Many writings get bogged down with heavy, fancy, and unnecessary terms. Information is presented here in a simple, straight-forward manner.

The first two parts of this book will give you information on basic money making tools and will tell you what to watch for and watch out for. Part Three offers a step-by-step guide for designing and using a custom made plan for wealth building action. Part Four is a dictionary of terms used in the world of money.

You should read the first three parts of this book and acquaint yourself with the dictionary in Part Four. There is no need to try to memorize the information in this book sentence-by-sentence. Just read the material through and get the general idea. This book will also serve as a handy reference —just return to it as needed as you proceed toward your money making goals.

PART ONE

In Pursuit of Wealth

CHAPTER 1

Wealth as a Goal

Everyone wants to be rich. The ultimate dream and goal of countless millions is to be wealthy. We work and work, scheme and plan, and hope that someday, somehow we will have piles and piles of money.

What is money? You give your time and talent in the workplace, and, in exchange, receive money. This money, in its convenient form, gives you the power to purchase what you want or need. Actually then, money in and of itself is not what we really want. The longing is actually for the things and the sense of well-being that money can bring. What we really want is to have what we want when we want it. Few would long enjoy staring at piles of green paper or shiny coins, but most would revel in the knowledge that almost any need or want could be instantly satisfied with the application of this money. The goal, then, is to have enough money to satisfy all present and future wants and needs. Once this is accomplished, you could then be called "wealthy."

How do you become wealthy? There are only a few ways this can happen: You may have been born into wealth, or you could marry a wealthy person—however, wealthy persons of the right gender are few and far between, and society frowns on marriage for the sole purpose of money—or, you might be extremely lucky and win your fortune. Lotteries, sweepstakes, and casinos all offer the promise of instant wealth.

But what if you were not born rich, do not marry wealth, or win? What is left? Think of this: In each wealthy family there was an ancestor who, with only a modest income, set aside a portion of it, put it into something he thought would increase in value, and succeeded. So, if you are not rich and want to be (or, yes, if you want to just be more comfortable), there is a method left—a do-it-yourself project. Wealth is more attainable than you may think, no matter how bad you view your current situation. It is a building process, bit by bit, step by step with each step bringing you closer to the goal.

Most people already have the first two basic ingredients required for a successful wealth building project; that is, most are able to generate at least a modest income and most can set aside a part of this income, even though it may be a very small part. However, every successful program has one additional ingredient. This absolutely essential ingredient is *knowledge*.

Your do-it-yourself wealth building program is headed for success when you have this knowledge. This knowledge includes knowing the money system of which we are all a part. It includes knowing the forces which affect the system so you can anticipate and adjust to them. And, it includes knowing choices and selecting the best one or ones for your particular needs and circumstances. This book is your foundation for all that knowledge. In it you will find the information you will need to proceed toward your wealth building goal.

In Part One, we will cover some of the important forces which you should understand and watch. These forces have a strong influence on the money system. They are very important. We will talk about the money tools the system makes available to you. These money tools are what you must use to construct your wealth building program. You do not need to use all of them; just choose the one or several which will be most beneficial to you. You will be able to make a good choice when you have a good knowledge of what is available and possible. This knowledge is provided in Part Two. In Part Three we will cover some tips, tactics, and techniques to use when selecting or using money tools—this will be *your* wealth building guide. And, finally, in Part Four you will find a Quick Reference Dictionary of money terms which can be used as a memory jogger or to explain a term you may have missed.

It will be helpful if you imagine your wealth building project as just that—a building program. You are going to actually build a structure. This structure will support all your hopes and dreams because it is made of wealth. Once built, the structure will provide the money for all your present and future needs and wants. You will have your own custom made wealth "building."

In constructing your building, you must consider the weather that it will have to withstand. The money system, within which you will operate, has many forces acting on it similar to weather. These forces can be destructive or of little consequence depending on how well you understand them and how well you've planned for them. The following section will give you the necessary information to help you successfully weather the storm.

CHAPTER 2

Hazards to Wealth Building

Inflation

Like an unpredictable wind, inflation can be just a breeze that ruffles your hair, or it can be the cutting edge of a storm laying waste to anything unprotected. So many well laid and carefully executed plans have ended in failure because of it. Let's get some protection by learning what it is and how it affects your program.

Inflation is simply rising prices; it is caused by too much money chasing too few goods. When the system has more money than it needs to run smoothly and grow, prices increase. Ideally, there should be just enough money in circulation to cover the amount of goods and services in the system. Exactly how much money is needed to keep everything running smoothly is extremely difficult to figure.

Inflation works like this: Too much money causes price increases. Price increases mean we must earn more to cover the cost of living. As we earn more, our taxes increase, so we must earn even more. Our employers must pay higher wages for us and other employees to stay even. To remain profitable, employers must charge more for goods and services; thus, more price increases. Round and round it goes; how to control it nobody knows. One thing is certain: Prices will increase and you *must* account for this inflation in your wealth building program.

It is very revealing to look at the history of inflation as measured by the *Consumer's Price Index (CPI)*. The CPI is reported by the U.S. Department of Labor and is based on prices of certain goods and services. A table of this inflation measurement is provided below. These figures reveal that during the last ten years, inflation has increased prices by an *average* of 9.21% per year. In other words, the purchasing power of every dollar you have has decreased by 9.21% every year for the last ten years. What the future rate will be is anybody's guess; however, the rate will probably fluctuate wildly as it has in the past.

PRICE INCREASE PERCENTAGES (INFLATION)

Compiled by U.S. Department of Labor

YEAR	PERCENTAGE
1982	3.9
1981	7.1
1980	11.8
1979	12.8
1978	9.2
1977	6.9
1976	3.7
1975	6.6
1974	18.3
1973	11.8

Because the recent inflation rate has been lower is no reason to believe that future rates will continue to be low. Note the wide variation in the rate. There is *no* way to predict inflation reliably because there are so many variable factors which can influence it. It is enough just to realize that inflation will change, and regardless of the changing values, it will have a strong impact on your wealth building program. Consider this: a 7% inflation rate cuts the purchasing power of your dollar *in half* in only ten years. A 14% rate halves your dollar in five years. At a minimal 3.5% rate of inflation, prices will double in only 20 years, and your money will be worth only half of what it is today. Inflation has been, is, and will continue to be an important force in the money system.

Interest Rates

Another force at work in the money system is called interest. Basically, **interest** is the rent charged for the use of money. It is very much like the sun. The economy needs to have a minimum amount, but too much can cause serious consequences. Interest makes lending profitable; however, rates that are too high bring the economy to a standstill as we saw in 1982.

If you are a saver and, therefore, can be a lender, interest is a good thing because you can receive this "rent" on saved money. However, this is true only up to a point. Again, like the sun, too much interest for too long can be damaging to your wealth. The high rates you may be receiving must be paid by borrowers. Many will not be able to pay the high rates and will not make purchases. Without loans to make purchases there may be no need for your talents, and there goes your income. Therefore, interest rates can be a boon to your wealth building, or they can cause it to go bust.

Interest rates, like inflation, are impossible to predict. Wide variations have occurred in the past and will continue to occur in the future. Some say to watch inflation to foresee interest rates; others watch interest rates to forecast inflation. The argument is similar to the age-old riddle of which came first, the chicken or the egg. It is enough to realize that these two forces, inflation and interest rates, are at work in the money system and must be included in your wealth building program.

Taxes

The third force, which strongly affects the money system, is taxes. Taxes are necessary to pay the cost of government. The government provides the things we cannot provide as individuals—defense of our system, public works, law and order, etc. All must be paid for.

Taxes are something like rain; a little is O.K. You probably will complain and be gloomy while you pay taxes, but as long as they do not take too much and the rain does not last, everything is all right.

The tax laws you operate under are called progressive. A **progressive tax** is one which charges a larger percentage of your earnings as your earnings increase. The more you earn, the more you are taxed.

There are two things certain about taxes: First, they will always be there, and second, they will change in size. Lawmakers may increase taxes to fight inflation, decrease them to fight recession, or change them to encourage or discourage this or that. The changes may be in different forms, shapes, or sizes, but taxes will be there chipping away at your income.

With these facts in mind, you are now well-armed. You know that the hazards threatening your wealth building—inflation, interest rates and taxes—are powerful forces. Your ability to recognize and react to these forces will help make your wealth building program successful. Let's turn now to money tools and the reasons you need to know about them.

PART TWO

Getting to Know the Tools of The World of Money

CHAPTER 3

The Need for Knowledge

To make wise choices about money tools, you must know what is available and you must understand the language of the world of money. Too often, writers assume the reader already has a background in the language. For example, a headline may read, "Money Market Vehicles Provide Record Yields." This would be meaningless to anyone who does not understand what a "Money Market Vehicle" is. Some may know that the money market is some vague place for invested money. But where is it? Should you invest there? How can you invest there? How does it work? And what, besides a traffic signal, is a yield?

Or...You decide that your wealth building program would benefit from some stock purchases. You locate a broker (stock salesperson) and then can only stare blankly as the broker talks about "an initial offering of a cumulative preferred stock" or a "debenture that is selling at a deep discount." Unless you know the language, the world of money can be a very strange sounding and frustrating place.

Equally as important as knowing the language is knowing that choices exist. If, in money jargon, the "yields" on "Money Market Vehicles" are no longer at attractive "record" levels, what else is available? The Capital Market may be the answer. Before you can decide, however, you must first know that the Capital Market exists.

You must know the language and choices well enough to make good decisions. Too often, a money tool is chosen simply because it is the most convenient or the closest at hand, so you end up trying to drive a large nail with a tack hammer, and you go through the motions but not much happens. When choosing money tools, ask yourself: What were the tools designed to do? How do you handle them to avoid damage or injury? Where can you find these tools? Can you afford them? Can you afford not to use them? All such questions need answers if the proper tool selection is to be made.

The following chapters will give you this type of information about money tools. After you have digested this information, you should be able to reject the tack hammer and select a heavy, well balanced, professional nail driving hammer to drive your nails and proceed more surely toward your money making goals.

Let's begin now, to make some sense out of all of this and to explore your choices. Let's turn first to an easy-to-understand explanation of the tools in the world of money. Later, we will discover some time-proven methods of using the tools to construct a wealth building to match your wildest dreams.

As we go along, do not try to memorize the passages as if you were studying for an exam; just get the gist! You will want to refer back to this book from time to time to refresh your memory.

CHAPTER 4

Stocks

Today, stock is probably the most popular tool used in the pursuit of money goals. The stock market has regularly set new records for the most shares ever bought and sold. The value of all traded stock shares has broken through previous highs, time after time. Everyone who successfully pursues wealth building will use this stock tool sooner or later. Some use this tool exclusively; however, most will include other tools as well as stocks in their wealth program. The strong attraction of stock is its ability to increase in value and dividends faster than the rate of inflation. There are stories about some spectacular successes. For example, a person who had bought 100 shares of a company called Computing-Tabulating-Recording Company back in 1915 for $2,800, would have seen the name changed to IBM, and the investment grow to over $20,000,000 (million) now.

So now, realizing that stock is a good tool to use in fighting inflation and that it can lead to fantastic wealth, you may be inclined to rush to the nearest stockbroker and buy some. But which stock will you buy? How do you recognize the IBMs? What is the meaning of all those terms used by the stockbroker? What—is a stock?!?

If you investigate the meaning of the word **stock**, you will find that it stands for the transferable certificates which provide evidence of a share of ownership in a corporation. In other words, when you own some of the stock of a corporation, you own part of that corporation. You have *not* simply loaned your money to the company—you have bought a piece of it.

This idea of ownership is important for your understanding of stocks. With a loan, you would have the promise of receiving the exact loaned amount back at some future date—plus, you may also receive some payments of rent (interest). When you buy stock, there is no such promise. If the company does well, your share of the business will be worth much more than you paid for it; if it does not do well, your share could be worth much less. In other words, you directly share in the future of the corporation, be it profitable or not.

Common Stock

How does this money tool called stock work? Exactly what is this mysterious device, and why would a business want to sell part ownerships of itself? How does this practice get started and what keeps it going? The following story about a fictitious company will help take some of this mystery out of stocks.

Irving R. Smart, a computer analyst, invented a simplified computer and had it patented. The booming interest in computer use assured him of a good market for his product. He found that in order to rent space, buy equipment and parts, hire workers, and sell his computers he would need $100,000. He had only $20,000 of his own. When he approached banks for a loan they refused. Banks are very cautious and seldom loan to new businesses just starting and without a proven record of success.

Irving decided to form a corporation and share the ownership (sell stock) to raise the needed money. The Smart Computers Corporation was formed by Irving and four friends who each provided $20,000. As evidence of joint ownership, each received a certificate for 1,000 shares (each costing $20) of stock in the corporation.

This new corporation would now be classified as a *privately owned* corporation—it still involved just the original five members—and the shares of stock held by one owner could not normally be sold or traded without the agreement of the other owners. Privately owned company stock is not available to the general public. Usually, as was the case with

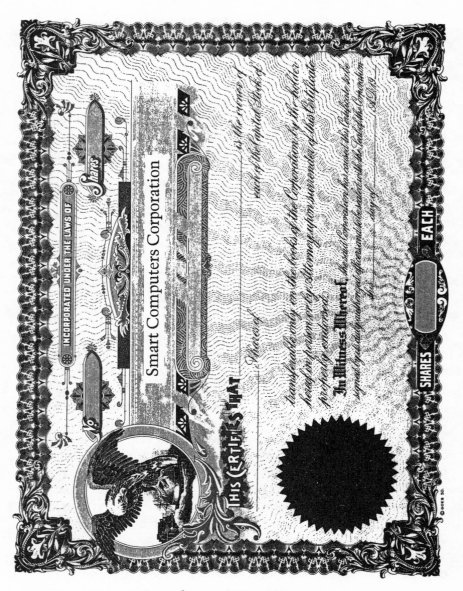

Sample Stock Certificate

our example company, privately owned corporations sell their stock to friends, relatives, and the like. But Smart Computers Corporation was destined for bigger and better times, as we shall see.

Sales of the new Smart computer were fantastic. The new company saw the need to increase its manufacturing to satisfy unfilled orders. To raise money for the needed expansion, Smart wanted the corporation to "go public," i.e., offer common stock for sale to the general public—the company would then be classified as *publicly held*. However, this move worried Smart's four friends who had put up the funds necessary to start the business. Smart soothed their worries by explaining what their situation would be as stockholders in a publicly owned corporation.

First, Smart outlined several basic rights that *all* owners of common stock have.

(1) Stockowners have the right to sell or trade their shares without the agreement of others. The stock is readily transferable to anyone wishing to purchase it. It can even be given and received as a gift.

(2) Stockowners usually have the right to maintain their proportionate share of the corporation. For example: Each owner of Smart Computers Corporation owns 1/5 of the company. If the company now offers 5,000 new shares of stock, each prior owner would have the first chance to buy 1/5 of the new stock or 1,000 shares each. This right assures stockholders that their ownership will not decrease against their will. The prior owners can refuse to purchase these new shares, but they are offered the opportunity to buy before the stock is offered to the public. This right is called **pre-emptive right.**

(3) Stockowners have the right to a share of the company's earnings—when and if the company decides to pay out any profits. This pay out would be in proportion to the number of shares owned—so much per share.

(4) Stockowners have the right to company property in case of bankruptcy. After all other debts have been paid, they receive payment in proportion to the number of shares owned.

(5) Stockowners have voting rights (unless nonvoting is specifically stated on the stock certificate). They can cast one vote for each share of stock owned; they can vote on major company issues and/or for elections of company directors.

Most of the time stockholders can not be present at meetings for these elections; therefore, they receive a proxy statement which they can fill out and mail to register their vote. A **proxy statement** is simply a legal device they can use to choose someone (a proxy) to vote for them.

(6) They would have the right to review company records. These records may be minutes of meetings and lists of stockholders. This right is not normally exercised unless serious problems develop.

(7) The stockholders have no financial obligation to the corporation. In other words, if the corporation were to incur debts and were unable to pay these debts, it could *not* ask stockholders for any payment. A statement to this effect is written on the face of stock certificates.

Smart was correct when he told his stockholders that knowledge of their rights was important. All buyers of common stock should be aware of the rights they have when they purchase ownership in a company. Smart then went on to outline his specific plan for the proposed public sale of stock.

Smart Computers Corporation through various methods would offer 1,000 new shares of common stock to each of five new investors. The new shares would sell for $25 apiece. Smart reminded the current stock holders that they had paid only $20 a share for their stock. Smart had consulted experts and had been assured that the new stock would easily sell at the $25 price. The experts were sure of this because Smart Computers was now a more proven company with a ready market that should assure rapid growth possibilities. The new investors were eager to purchase this opportunity for growth. This sale of new stock would add $125,000 to the original investment of $100,000. Even if the original owners did not buy any of the new stock, which they had the right to do, they would gain. The original five owners had shared total ownership of a $100,000 company; after the sale of the new stock, they collectively would own half of a company worth $225,000. Each would make a profit of $2,500 ($100,000 ÷ 5 = $20,000 initial investment; $225,000 ÷ 10 = $22,500), at least on paper, and all approved of the plan to "go public."

The new shares sold to five new investors; each purchased 1,000 shares. Smart Computers Corporation now had 10 stockholders—10 part-owners. It would not be practical to

INTEREST RATES DECLINE

GRAND OPENING

GET YOURS NOW!!!!

MARY'S FLOWER SHOP

NEW COMPUTER FIRM GOES PUBLIC

A new, fast-growing computer manufacturing company, Smart Computers Corporation, now offers shares of its common stock to the public. Their new abbreviated name is SCC and they have been increasing sales by 123% per year.

STOCK MARKET SETS NEW RECORD

try to run a business with 10 bosses so they elected a board of directors and named Irving as the president of the company. Once a year there would be a meeting open to all stockholders; everyone could learn how the business was doing and could vote on certain matters.

During the first years, the investors received no pay out of company profits. All the corporation's earnings were being plowed back into the business to provide for continued growth. However, all stockholders like to receive pay outs of profits (known as **dividends**), and in the third year, there was a profit of $40,000. Therefore, the board of directors decided to pay $10,000 of these profits to investors. The board announced (declared) that a dividend of $1 was to be paid to the holder of every share. The remaining $30,000 of profit was retained by the corporation for further expansion.

This dividend action of SCC is typical of young, growing companies. Their stock normally pays only small or sometimes no dividends because most of the earnings are kept to enable further growth. More mature companies normally pay a regular and often steadily increasing dividend. Dividends can be paid in dollars or in the form of additional shares of stock.

Some stockholders now wanted to sell some of their stock to collect the profits these shares represented. At the same time, they wanted to remain as stockholders to share in the expected future growth. These stockholders were worried about their ability to sell some of their shares because the corporation was prospering, and now each share was worth a lofty sum. There were very few people who could afford to buy at such a high price. It was then decided by the board of directors to **split** the stock 100 for 1. (This is not a normal split.) This meant that for every share of original stock, the company would issue 100 new shares. Each new share would be worth only one-hundredth as much as each old share, but each stockholder had 100 times as many shares. The new shares could be more easily sold at the lower price. In addition, the stock would now qualify for listing on a major stock exchange (such as the New York Stock Exchange), and listing would further add to the ease of selling shares. (Note: To qualify for listing on most major exchanges, a corporation must have at least one million shares of stock—Smart Computers now qualified—100 × 10,000 original shares = one million shares.) The original stockholders could now take some of their profits by selling some of their stock and still retain a portion of their original ownership.

When some investors decided to sell some of their stock, they went to a stock salesperson known as a **broker.** The broker had already received requests for the stock from other investors and quickly arranged the sale of the shares. The broker received two fees (commissions) for his service—one paid by the buyer and one paid by the seller—and the stockholders selling shares made a handsome profit. The new stockholders buying the shares had all the rights we previously discussed which come with stock ownership. They could also benefit from future growth of the stock's price and receive any future dividends. Smart Computers Corporation received none of the monies involved in these exchanges. The only time a company gets money for its stock is when the stock is a **primary issue,** i.e., when the stock is first offered for sale by the company. A company can offer many primary issues, at various times. When stock is traded after the primary issue, it is known as a secondary offering. The **secondary offering** occurs when stockowners decide to sell their shares. All monies go to them—not to the company.

STOCK VALUE

The investors in Smart Computers Corporation had chosen well because the value of the corporation's stock had increased steadily. A stock's value can be measured in different ways. Most stock certificates come with a value printed on the face of the certificate. This is called the **par value.** A stock's par value is usually stated as an even figure such as $1, $10, etc. and has no meaning except to the company's accountant who must keep track of outstanding shares.

Another method of measurement is called **book value.** If, for some reason, Smart Computers Corporation stopped doing business, locked the doors, sold all equipment and parts, and paid all their bills, the remaining money would be known as the company's book value. The corporation's accountants keep track of this value in their books, and hence the name.

THE DAILY BLAH

STOCK MARKET SURGES

GET YOUR STEREO STUFF AT STEPHEN'S STEREO STORE

HOUSING STARTS RISE

FIRM WINS LISTING ON NYSE

Smart Computers Corporation stock can now be traded through the New York Stock Exchange. SCC stock has grown steadily and reflects the high demand for the new Smart Computer. The stock's price can be followed by watching for the SCC symbol in the stock listings for the NYSE in this paper.

Let's assume that Smart Computers has a book value of $1 million and it has one million shares of stock. Each share of stock would then have claim to $1 worth of the company's debt-free property—the book value per share would be $1. A third measurement of stock value called market value is much more significant than either of the above.

Market value is the price the stock would sell for today. This price is based largely on expectations. If buyers strongly believe the corporation will prosper, its stock price will be higher; if the buyers have doubts about the future of the company, the price will be lower. This market value has no logical relationship to book value. Many stocks sell for prices below book value and many more sell at prices far above book value. Market value will vary with changes in the general economy, other similar stock prices, or anything which affects the buyer's belief in the future of the company. The prospects for the future of Smart Computers Corporation are very good—it has just paid its first dividend, its earnings have been steadily growing, and it has made known its plans for expansion—therefore, the current market value of its stock far exceeds its book value.

COMMON STOCK VALUES

TERM	DESCRIPTION	USE
Par Value*	Printed on the stock certificate.	A useless value.
Book Value*	The debt-free value, divided by the number of shares, of everything the company owns.	May be used for stock comparisons.
Market Value*	The last price the stock sold for. This price is the one quoted in the media.	This is the only "real" measurement of a stock's current worth.

*All terms are normally quoted as a price per share.

The increases in the market value of Smart Computers Corporation (SCC) stock were a reflection of the steadily increasing demand for its product. So, now there was a need for further expansion. The board of directors decided to issue more stock to raise the monies needed for this expansion; however, they had to be sure that the pre-emptive rights of their current stockholders were protected. As you recall, a pre-emptive right affords stockholders the right to maintain their percent of ownership in the company by offering them the first opportunity to purchase new stock. Therefore, SCC issued rights certificates to all current stockholders at the same time that they offered their new primary issue of common stock to the public. Each existing stockholder would then have the opportunity to buy the new stock at a set price. Usually, **rights certificates** offer the new stock at a price below the current market value of the old stock. Therefore, rights certificates have a market value of their own and can be bought and sold the same as common stock. For example, if SCC stock were selling for $50 (market value), the rights certificate might offer the new shares at $45 each. The holder of the certificate could then either buy the new stock at $45 a share or sell the certificate to another investor. Rights certificates are usually short-lived, and the holder must exercise the right (purchase the new stock) within a specified time, usually less than a month.

Warrants work the same as rights certificates. A company can offer rights or warrants at any time to encourage stock sales. Whereas rights certificates usually expire within a month, warrants can have a life of several years.

The stock we have been discussing thus far at Smart Computers Corporation is known as common stock. It simply represents a partial ownership of the business. Common stock owners have certain rights such as voting and pre-emptive rights. Stock value can be measured in many ways. Two common ways of expressing stock value are: book value, i.e., the value of debt-free assets owned by the company; and market value, the price, based upon the future of the company, that a buyer is willing to pay (and seller willing to accept). A corporation may decide on a stock split. In the event of a stock split, the company will exchange a stated number of new shares for each old share, for example, 2-for-1. Common stockholders may also receive any declared dividends or pay-outs of company profits when the corporation's board of directors believes it is appropriate. Let's return now to Smart's business to see what is developing.

Preferred Stock

The expansion of Smart's company was completed on schedule. But then Smart was offered the opportunity to buy out a competitor and so—you guessed it—the corporation needed more money, and it decided to issue more stock to pay for the acquisition. However, this time it issued preferred stock. The board of directors decided on preferred because it appeals to a different type of investor, and this would help assure a ready market for the new offering. Selling more common stock would probably seriously decrease the common's market value due to oversupply.

The type of investors interested in **preferred stocks** are usually looking for less risk and an assured income from dividends. The amount of dividends paid to preferred stockholders is stated on the certificate and can not change. Like common stock, preferred represents an actual share in the ownership of the company; however, preferred does not normally have voting rights. Unlike common stock, the *par value* stated on the face of the certificate of preferred stock *is* important. It is the amount used to calculate the percentage of the dividend. For example, a 6% preferred stock with a par value of $100 would pay a $6 yearly dividend (.06 × $100 = $6). Dividends are usually paid quarterly. In the above example, $1.50 would be paid every 3 months to the holder of every share. Many preferred stocks are issued with a par value of $100 per share; however, some preferreds are issued without any par value (no-par). In these cases, the dividend is stated as a dollar figure ($6 no-par preferred). The market value of all preferred stock is determined by supply and demand and the public's opinion of the company's future.

Preferred dividends must be paid before any dividends can be paid to common stockholders; and thus, preferred stockholders are more assured of receiving the promised dividends.

Also, preferred stock has a higher claim on company property than common stock, i.e., preferred is senior to common stock. If the company were to go out of business, preferred stockholders would be paid before common stockholders as the names imply.

The predictable dividends make preferred stock very desirable. The dividends remain the same regardless of fluctuations in the market value of the stock. The company will pay the dividends based on the face amount (par value) of the stock certificate. If the face amount of the certificate is $100 and investors are only willing to pay $90, the company will still pay the dividend based on $100.

Companies can issue preferred stocks with a variety of attractive features. Most preferred stock has at least one of several added attractions. One such attraction is called cumulative preferred. If the company can not pay the promised dividend on a **cumulative preferred** stock, the unpaid dividend will be added to the next year's dividend and will be paid before any dividends go to common stockholders.

Another added attraction of some preferred stock is called **convertibility.** With this attractive feature, the owner can exchange (convert) a share of convertible for a stated number of common stock shares anytime during a stated time period (often five years). For example, if Smart's common stock was selling for $45 a share and he issued convertible preferred at $100 a share, it would carry the provision that each share (of preferred) could be exchanged for two shares of common stock during the next five years. If the market value of the common stock increased *past* $50 a share, the $100 convertible preferred stock would be more valuable because of the two-for-one exchange privilege.

Preferred stock can have an attractive feature called **participation.** With this feature, the dividends of preferred generally keep pace with those of regular common stock, i.e., if common stock dividends increase, so do those of the participating preferred.

The latest development in added attractions for preferred stock is the **adjustable-rate preferred.** (Hang in there...we're almost through with stocks!!) The dividend on standard preferred is a set amount, as we discussed above. This new adjustable-rate feature allows the company to periodically adjust the dividends. (Quarterly adjustments are common.) The amount of dividend is based on the rates of treasury issues (bonds, bills, and/or notes). (See the section on Money Market.) This adjustable feature enables preferred to keep pace with rapidly changing interest rates, be they high or low.

PREFERRED STOCK "EXTRA ADDED ATTRACTIONS"

ATTRACTIONS	BENEFITS
Cumulative	If the company can not pay the promised dividend, the unpaid amount is added to the next dividend.
Convertible	A share of preferred can be exchanged for a set number of common stock shares.
Participating	The dividend can be increased to keep pace with any increases in the company's common stock dividend.
Adjustable Rate	The dividend can be changed by the company by using a set formula to match current market interest rates. This feature would be attractive when interest rates are rising rapidly.

Note: Preferred stock can have none, one, some, or all of these attractions. The greater the number, the more attractive the stock!

Smart Computers Corporation (SCC) decided to issue a preferred stock (Class A, since this was the first batch of preferred they offered) which paid a 7% fixed dividend every year noncumulative. SCC's new preferred had the convertible feature and could be exchanged for two shares of common stock during the next five years.

New investors eagerly bought this new issue of preferred stock because they could now share the ownership of a prosperous and promising business, and at the same time they would receive a portion of the profits in the form of the fixed

SMART COMPUTERS OFFERS NEW PREFERRED

Smart Computers Corporation announced a new offering of 7% preferred stock. The stock, par $100, is convertible into two shares of SCC common, and the dividend is noncumulative. The firm has been growing rapidly, and the price of its common stock has doubled in the last year. Sales of the new preferred have been brisk.

NEW INVESTMENT GUIDE MAKES INVESTING SIMPLE
MAKE MONEY MAKE MONEY

CURTIS' COSMIC CORNER

AUTO SALES SHOW GOOD GAINS

dividend. They also could trade their shares of preferred for common stock if the market value of the common increased to an amount that would make the trade profitable.

As we have just seen, preferred stock can be very desirable, especially if it has some of the extra added attractions. Convertible preferreds have the best of both (common and preferred) worlds: They have fixed dividends, the added security of a senior claim on company property, and the opportunity for faster growth by converting to common stock. Preferred stock is commonly known as a fixed income investment because the dividends received from it are stated when issued and can not change—they're predictable. (Two exceptions to this are the participating and the new adjustable-rate preferreds.) Remember, the more added attractions, the better the preferred will be.

Note: You now know about the two types of stock—common stock and preferred stock. All stock must be either common or preferred, but it may be grouped with other similar stocks. These groupings, referred to as either Blue Chip, Growth, Income, or Special Situation stocks, are defined in Part Four under the general term "stock."

CHAPTER 5

Bonds

This major wealth building tool that we will discuss has a popularity second only to stocks. It is designed for those who are unable or unwilling to take the larger degree of risk found in stocks. A **bond** is simply a certificate stating that the bondholder has loaned money to an organization. Bonds have a higher safety of principal (the amount invested), than do stocks, i.e., investors are more assured of getting back the exact amount invested. Also, bondholders are assured of receiving a set amount of earnings. These earnings are called **interest** and are actually rent that the bondholders receive for their money. When investors buy bonds, they simply loan their money for a set time period and receive an unchangeable (fixed) amount of annual interest. They will receive the percent stated on the bond certificates.

All bonds are issued with a stated interest rate payable twice a year. The rate of interest is often called the **coupon rate.** Although less common now, some bonds are still issued with coupons attached to the certificate itself. Each coupon represents an interest payment. Bondholders present one of these coupons to receive their payment of interest. These types of bonds are called **bearer bonds.** The name comes from the fact that the interest will be paid to whoever carries (bears) the coupon to the paying agent; there is no registered owner's name.

More commonly bonds are a type called **registered bonds.** With this type, the name of the bond's owner is recorded by the company and the interest payments are sent directly to him.

When investors buy bonds, they loan their money to an organization for a specific length of time. The date is printed on the certificate. This date is called the **maturity date** and is the date the company promises to pay back the exact amount loaned by bondholders. Maturity dates will vary. Smaller companies generally issue shorter maturity dates, perhaps as short as 10 years; larger companies may issue bonds which will not mature for 30 years. The pay back process is called redeeming. The organization will **redeem** the bonds on such-and-such a date.

Bonds are usually issued at a price of $1,000 each. This is known as the par value or **face value,** since it is the price printed on the face or front of the bond certificate. After the initial issue, the market value of bonds may be more or less than the par value. The market value will fluctuate according to the willingness of investors to loan monies at the bond's interest rate. Bonds are said to be selling at a **premium** when the market value is higher than the par value. When the market value is lower than par, the bonds will sell at a **discount.** For example, the original buyer of a $1,000 bond paying 10% interest can resell this bond for $1,000 (par value) as long as the interest available in other places is approximately 10%. However, if general market interest rates are now around 12%, the bondholder will have to reduce the price of his bond (sell at a discount) to find a willing buyer. The reverse holds true also: If market interest rates decline under 10%, the bondholder can get more (a premium) than $1,000 for his bond. In general, bond market values move in the opposite direction of market interest rates.

Even though market interest rates play the major role in determining the market value of a bond, many other factors also influence this price. If there is a change in the company's ability to pay the interest or in its ability to redeem the bond at maturity, the bond's price will reflect it. Changes in the purchasing power of the dollar (inflation, deflation) will also affect market value. Remember, regardless of how much the market value may fluctuate, the bond owner will get back the exact amount he paid for the bond at maturity. All he needs to do is hold on and collect the interest.

BOND FEATURES

Par Value—The face amount or price printed on bond certificates. Interest payments are based on this amount.

Interest Rate—Stated on the bond certificate as a percentage, this is the amount of "rent" you will receive for your loaned money.

Maturity Date—The date the company promises to pay back loaned amounts.

Bearer Bonds*—Anyone who presents the bond or bond coupon will be paid.

Registered Bonds*—The owner is recorded and payments will be sent to the owner.

---

*All bonds are either Bearer or Registered bonds.

You are now familiar with the general characteristics of bonds. Let's return to the adventures of Smart Computers Corporation and explore a type of bond called the corporate bond.

Corporate Bonds

Smart Computers Corporation (SCC) had grown steadily, and demand for its computers was still exceeding its ability to produce them. SCC now wanted to purchase some suitable land and build its own plant rather than rent more space. It needed to raise a large sum of money, larger than any one bank was willing to loan. And yet, SCC did not want to further increase its number of owners by issuing more stock. Therefore, it decided to issue corporate bonds to raise the needed monies.

Corporate bonds are loans to companies and have all the general characteristics we just discussed. Corporate bonds, however, may have two additional features. They may be convertible or callable or both. **Convertible bonds** operate the same as convertible preferred stock, i.e., they may be exchanged for a set number of common stock shares. If bonds are **callable,** the issuing companies are allowed to redeem the bonds (buy them back) before the maturity date. The term call stems from the ability of companies to "call in" the bonds for redemption. All bonds will either be callable or noncallable. If bonds are callable, there will be a call price and time limit printed on the bonds. The call price will be higher than the par value. For example, the bond may be redeemed at $1,025 even though the par value is only $1,000. The time limit might be stated as a date five years from the date of issue.

SCC had to decide among several types of corporate bonds. One type is called a debenture. Don't let that fancy name scare you; a **debenture** (pronounced di-ben'-cher) is simply a large size I.O.U. There is no specific real property pledged against this type of bond. The general credit worthiness of the corporation is enough security for these bonds. A debenture is the type of bond most frequently issued by most large, well-known industrial firms. Another bond is called a **subordinated debenture.** This is simply an I.O.U. (a debenture) which has to wait until other existing bonds are paid before it can receive its due. (It is subordinate to other bonds.) If there are not enough funds to pay everyone, holders of this bond only have claim to any remaining funds.

Another type of corporate bond is the **mortgage bond.** This bond is secured by specific corporate property such as a building or land. A mortgage bond is known as a senior security, since it has first claim on property. The property which is used to back up (secure) a corporation's mortgage bond will normally be worth more than the value of the bonds for which it is pledged. This is an added safety feature. It assures that even in a bankruptcy sale, the property would bring in at least enough to pay bondholders. If the company were to dissolve, mortgage bondholders would be paid before other bondholders (such as debenture bondholders) or stockholders.

Two other types of bonds similar to mortgage bonds are the Equipment Trust Certificate and the Collateral Trust Bonds. The **Equipment Trust Certificates** are issued by transportation companies such as airlines and railroads. The property used to secure these certificates are the company's aircraft or railroad cars and/or engines. The **Collateral Trust Bonds** are issued by companies which own the stocks and bonds of other companies. These securities would then be pledged to back up (used as collateral) the Collateral Trust

Bonds. In this case, the pledged securities must have a market value of at least 25% more than the face value of the bonds.

The rules governing the issuance of bonds with property pledged as security are complicated and complex. It is enough to know that all the rules are designed to protect you, the bondholder—and not the company. The rules restrict what the company can and can not do with the pledged property and set specific procedures to protect the bondholders.

CORPORATE BOND TYPES

Debenture—A giant I.O.U.

Subordinated Debenture—A giant I.O.U. with less priority than other bonds.

Mortgage Bonds—Backed by the pledge of property.

Equipment Trust Certificates—Backed by the pledge of rolling stock such as aircraft or railroad cars.

Collateral Trust Bonds—Backed by the pledge of stocks and bonds.

Note

• Some corporate bonds may be *callable*, i.e., the company would have the right to redeem them before maturity.

• Some corporate bonds may be *convertible*, i.e., the bonds may be exchanged for a set number of shares of the company's common stock.

• Some bonds may be both *callable* and *convertible*.

Smart Computers Corporation (SCC) decided to issue convertible 7% debenture bonds maturing in 20 years. Each bond could be traded for 40 shares of SCC common stock anytime after five years. SCC also included a call provision effective after five years. This meant it could redeem the bonds before the maturity date but not before five years had passed.

This bond issue had many advantages for both the new investors and the corporation. The convertible feature made it particularly attractive. Investors could assure themselves of a 7% interest rate with a strong company behind it, and at the same time, have the possibility of sharing in the future gains made by SCC common stock. If SCC common continued to increase its market value as it had done thus far, in five years the value of 40 shares would far exceed the par value ($1,000) of the bond. Investors could then convert their bonds and make a handsome profit by selling the common stock.

Smart Computers Corporation liked the convertible feature, also. The business saw this feature as a possible means of reducing its debt without the need for cash: If bondholders converted the bonds for common stock, there would be no need to redeem them at maturity. This convertible feature also meant that the bond issue could be sold at a lower interest rate than one without this feature. For example, the experts had told SCC that a straight debenture bond (backed only by the credit worthiness of the company) would have to offer an 8% interest rate. The convertible feature would assure bond sales at only 7%. This 1% savings in interest over the 20-year life of the bond would amount to millions of dollars. All convertible bonds offer an interest rate ½ to 1% lower than nonconvertibles.

Investors also liked the 20-year maturity. It meant that for the long term they could be assured of the interest income, and yet, they were sure of a pay back of the loan amount after a moderate 20 years. This maturity was good for the company because it allowed enough time to get the new plant operating and because it allowed enough time to bring in some profits which could be set aside to provide for redeeming the bonds, either at maturity or by exercising the call provision.

In review, corporate bonds, similar to the ones just issued by Smart Computers Corporation, are a good tool to choose when you need to have the safety and fixed income they offer. Remember that a bond is simply a certificate stating that you, the buyer, have loaned the company your money (usually a minimum of $1,000) and will receive a payment of so much interest semi-annually. You, as a bondholder, are a creditor of the company, and the company promises to pay you back, at the bond's maturity, the exact amount loaned. When selecting a particular corporate bond, you will be choosing from the different types we discussed, such as the debentures, the mortgage bonds, or the equipment or collateral trust certificates. You should be aware

September XX, 19XX **THE DAILY BLAH** Page 1B

SMART COMPUTERS' BOND A SELL-OUT!!

Smart Computers Corporation's issue of a 7% convertible debenture was sold-out in only four days! The new 20-year bonds, par $1,000, can be exchanged for SCC common stock. Smart Computers have been selling like hot cakes and the company's stocks have been very popular with investors. Their new bond proved to be equally popular and was rated AAA by Standard and Poor's.

MAN BITES DOG

JEANETTE'S GEMS OF WISDOM

PRESIDENT WILL SPEAK TO LOCAL SCOUTS

that special provisions can make a big difference between bonds. Two important provisions are convertibility and callability. Remember also that corporate bond market values will fluctuate, and if you want to sell a bond before maturity, you may not receive par value for it—you may receive a premium for your bond (more than par value) or you may have to sell at a discount (less than par value). Bond market values will vary in response to changes in the general economy, especially to changes in interest rates. Of course, par value can always be assured if the bond is held until maturity.

Smart Computers Corporation had to consider all the above factors when it decided on a specific type of bond. The bond had to be attractive because there is a lot of competition for investors who are looking for a relatively safe fixed income for the long run. And—there was another very attractive competitor. This competitor was a bond offered by local governments, a municipal bond. Let's see if this tool might be a good one for you.

Municipal Bonds

Municipal bonds have a special appeal as a wealth building tool because the income received from them (interest payments) is "tax-free," i.e., the income is exempt from federal income taxation. The federal government can not interfere with the conduct of the business of local governments. Taxing the interest paid by local governments to its bondholders is considered to be interference. Most municipal bonds are also free from state income taxes if the bond owner lives in the state where the bond is issued.

Today, this "tax-free" income is becoming important to more and more investors. Those who are considered to be wealthy have always sought this type of investment; however, the tax advantage offered by munies (municipal bonds) is appealing to more and more middle income families. These families find that their incomes have put them in the higher tax brackets. This happens when inflation artificially swells incomes or when families have two paychecks because the spouse also works outside the home. In these higher tax brackets, tax-free interest becomes an important investment consideration. (More on tax implications later.)

The municipal bond is very similar to the corporate bond. When you buy a municipal bond you are simply loaning your money to a local government, and in return, will receive a stated amount of interest, and your original investment will be paid back at the bond maturity date. Good decisions about municipal bonds depend on your familiarity with the different types of municipal bonds and some of their unique provisions.

Municipal bonds may be issued by any of the variety of local governmental units. States, counties, cities, housing authorities, school districts, or any agency of these governments may issue municipals. Anytime money is needed for projects for the good of the public, municipal bonds may be offered to raise the needed sums. In this way, many hospitals, roads, sewers, schools, etc. receive the money needed for construction and/or improvements.

Usually, the par value of a muni is $5,000, and the interest is slightly lower than rates available from other sources. Their "tax-free" status can more than make up for the lower interest rate, depending on your tax bracket. Maturity dates can range anywhere from 5 to 50 years.

There are several types of municipal bonds. The most common is called a **general obligation bond** and is closely related to the corporate debenture. This bond is backed only by the general credit worthiness and (most important) the taxing power of the government unit. The money for interest payments and eventual bond redemption comes from property taxes, sales taxes, or any tax of a general nature. Another type of muni is called a **special assessment bond.** It is different from the general obligation bond only because it will use special taxes to pay bond debts. These taxes are levied against only those who will use the project for which the bond was issued. For example, the users of a new sewer or a new school would pay this special tax to repay bondholders.

Still another type of municipal bond is called the **revenue bond.** This bond is issued when the project can expect to repay bondholders with earnings. Some examples of projects that issue this type of municipal bond are airports, rapid transit systems, college dorms, toll roads, bridges, and tunnels. These projects would use the income (the revenues) received from users to pay bond interest and retire the bond at maturity. A bond that is similar to the revenue bond is the **housing authority bond.** This bond is issued to raise money for the construction of public housing and will use the rents received from occupants to repay bondholders. In addition, these bonds are backed by the local government's public housing authority (PHA). The PHA guarantees that collected rents will be sufficient to cover bond interest payments and principal. If not, the local government will make up the difference through the PHA. Some of these issues are backed by the federal housing authority (FHA). FHA backed issues are the safest of all since the taxing power of the federal government is behind them.

There are three ways to issue bonds: in serial form, in straight term, or in series form. Most municipal bonds are **serial bonds.** Even though all the bonds are issued (sold) on the same date, there is a different maturity date assigned to different batches. This enables the bond issue to be redeemed a little at a time. Corporations may also issue serial bonds; however, most corporate bonds are straight **term bonds** with one issue date and one maturity date. Infrequently, corporate and/or municipal bonds are issued in a series. **Series bonds** have many primary issue dates; however, all bonds in the series have the same maturity date. This enables the bond issuer to receive monies over a *series* of dates, and therefore, pay interest only on money needed at specific times. These series bonds are sometimes used for construction projects which will last many years. The summary below should help keep these three ways of issuing bonds straight.

Serial Bonds—(municipal)—same issue date, different maturity dates.

Series Bonds—(infrequent)—different issue dates, same maturity date.

Term Bonds—(corporate)—same issue date, same maturity date.

You now have a good basic understanding of municipal bonds. They are simply documents that show that money has been loaned to local governmental units. Most have a par value of $5,000, and the interest is printed on the certificates as a percentage of this par value. Although the interest they pay is relatively low, they can be very desirable because this interest is federally tax free. The issuing government's credit and taxing power are behind the general obligation and special assessment bonds.

Revenue and housing authority bonds will collect fees to pay bondholders. The safest of all the bonds we have discussed are the housing authority bonds backed by the FHA. Federal backing for any investment represents the highest degree of safety. Let's look now at other investments offered by the federal government to the investor that needs a sure, fixed income.

Government Issues

Government issues may well be an important tool for your wealth building program. For one thing, they are an extremely safe investment. They are backed by the "full faith and credit" of the federal government. You can be sure that you will be paid because all the government needs to do, in effect, is to print more money. Government issues also have some special tax advantages. All federal issues are exempt from state and/or local income taxes, and some allow you to postpone payment of federal taxes on the interest.

Even though many of these government issues are spurned by some wealthy or "sophisticated" investors, government issues are very popular. At least one out of every ten dollars invested in this country is invested in government issues. Well over $70 billion worth of savings bonds alone are owned by millions of Americans. There are well over 10 million people enrolled in the payroll savings plan; however, there are many ways in which the different types of government issues may be purchased. Our discussion of government issues will begin with the most well-known— the U.S. Savings Bond.

U.S. SAVING BONDS

U.S. Savings Bonds, like other bonds, represent a loan of your money to the issuer, in this case the federal government.

In return for the loan, the government promises to pay interest and reimburse your principal. A significant difference from other bonds is the fact that savings bonds are not transferable, i.e., you can not sell them to someone else. They are a registered type of bond (the owner's name is recorded), and no provision is made for easy changes of ownership. Some of the popularity of U.S. Savings bonds comes from the ease of purchase (more than two-thirds of savings bond sales are from payroll deduction plans). Savings bonds are readily available where you work or from your bank.

There are two types of savings bonds—EE bonds and HH bonds (called double E and double H bonds). Savings bonds bought before 1979 were known by the single letter designation (E or H bonds). Lets consider the EE bonds first.

Series EE Savings Bonds come in values ranging from $50 to $10,000. They are sold at a 50% discount from their face value. For example, a $100 bond will cost you $50 dollars. At maturity, the owner can collect at least the full face value of the bond ($100 in the example). In other words, when you loan the federal government your money through a EE bond, your interest will be paid only when you redeem (sell back or cash in) the bond. The interest received from EE bonds is subject to federal income taxes but not to state and/or local income tax. However, the federal income tax is not normally payable until the interest is received when the bond is redeemed. Thus, EE bonds are a means of deferring this income tax (delaying the payment of tax on the interest). You may, however, elect to pay the tax as the interest is actually earned annually. This would be a good idea if a child is designated as the bond owner. EE bonds allow a maximum investment ceiling of $30,000 (face value) per year.

What rate of interest do EE bonds pay? That would seem to be a simple question, and the answer is important if you are going to wisely decide whether or not to use this money tool. However, the answer is elusive, and is usually presented in a very complicated manner. There is almost no current information easily available on savings bonds. Changes in these savings bond issues have been extensive, and there have been a large number of changes just since 1979. There is a noticeable reluctance at local banks to give out this information.

One can only guess that the reason for this is that the banks consider the savings bonds as competition for their own savings program. In any case, unless you live close to a Federal Reserve Bank, you will find current information on savings bonds to be scarce. Hopefully, this will soon change. But what is the current rate? It is explained below, as simply as possible.

EE savings bonds purchased after November 1, 1982, have a variable interest rate but will earn at least 7.5% annually. The 7.5% is actually a floor, and you will receive at least that amount if you hold the bond five years, or until maturity (10 years). In other words, you will receive a minimum of 7.5% interest on a bond cashed in anytime after five years. If you redeem a bond held for less than five years, you receive only 5.5%. After five years, a variable rate may be paid. This variable rate is based on the interest of treasury issues (See T-Bills in Money Market Chapter). After five years you will receive either a variable rate or 7.5%, whichever is higher. The table below should help to clarify this.

EE Savings Bonds*	
Length of Time Held	**Rate of Return**
**6 months–5 years	5.5%
5 years–10 years	7.5% OR a higher variable amount

*Bought after November 1, 1982.
**You must hold bonds 6 months before redemption.

EE bond maturity periods have been different for different batches of bonds sold during the past few years. The current 10-year maturity will probably remain in effect for a long time. Before, the government was changing maturity periods when it changed interest rates to keep the bonds competitive. Now, with the variable interest rate provision, there should be no need for further changes.

You need not redeem a EE bond at maturity. It will continue to earn interest at the current variable rate or 7.5%, whichever is higher. Some EE bonds sold before November 1, 1982, carried very nice, fixed interest rates (9%), and holding them past maturity may very well be a good idea. Compare them with current interest rates of other money tools.

The other type of savings bond is the **HH savings bond.** The only way to obtain one of these is by trading EE or E bonds for it. HH bonds come in denominations of $500 to $5,000; therefore, you must have at least $500 worth of E or EE bonds to trade. Series HH bonds are a tool designed for those who want the safety of a government bond and want interest to be paid to them as it is earned. The series HH bonds do this. Currently, they mature in 10 years and will pay an annual interest rate of 7.5% semi-annually. They must be held six months before redemption.

When E or EE bonds are exchanged for HH, the taxes that had been deferred on the E or EE will continue to be deferred. This is a good maneuver if you are in a high tax bracket when the E/EE bonds mature. Without the trade, you may loose a large chunk of your earned interest to taxes. By trading for HH bonds you can further defer the payment of these taxes, possibly until the lower tax brackets of retirement. When the HH bonds are finally sold, all deferred taxes will then be payable.

Savings bonds have a nice safety feature. If they are ever lost, stolen, or destroyed, they can be replaced. If you need to replace a bond, write to the address below and provide as much information as possible—registration number, date of purchase, place of purchase, name, address, and social security number of the owner. Keep this information separate from the bond storage place.

For savings bond replacement, write to:

> Bureau of the Public Debt
> 200 Third Street
> Parkersburg, West Virginia 26101

TREASURY ISSUES

Treasury bonds are sold in denominations of $1,000 to $1,000,000 and can be issued as either a bearer or registered bond. They are sold at face value and the interest is paid semi-annually. Their maturity dates range from 7 to 30 years. Treasury bonds are transferable; and therefore, like other transferable bonds, they have a changeable market value. For example, if general market interest rates go up, the market value of treasury bonds will decrease. Treasury issues can be bought at most banks and at all brokers.

The Treasury also issues **treasury notes.** The only difference between treasury notes and bonds is that the maturity of notes is shorter (only one to ten years), and the minimum sale is $10,000. These notes are generally sold in the bearer form.

A third type of treasury issue is called a **treasury bill.** These have even shorter maturities than notes and will be discussed in the money market section of this book. The table below will help you remember the various treasury issues.

Treasury Issues	Term	Maturity
Treasury Bills	short term	3 months to one year
Treasury Notes	medium term	1–10 years
Treasury Bonds	long term	7–30 years

GINNIE MAE

The last government issues to be considered as a tool are known by the nickname of **Ginnie Maes.** These certificates are issued by the Government National Mortgage Association (GNMA—GiNnie MAe) and, hence the name. The money to pay holders of these certificates comes from mortgages held by the federal government. When mortgage payments are made, they are passed through to holders of Ginnie Mae certificates. The GNMA backs up these payments, and if they are not received from the homeowners, GNMA pays them. Each holder receives a *monthly* payment for his invested money. This monthly payment is a very attractive feature for those living on this income.

The average life of GNMA issues is 12 years because this is the amount of time the average mortgage is held before it is paid off or refinanced. The owner does not, however, have to keep the certificate(s) for 12 years; they may be resold to others at anytime. Interest rates available on these Ginnie Maes have been the highest of all government issues but will vary from one Ginnie Mae issue to the next. The minimum investment in these Ginnie Mae pass-throughs is $25,000; however, you can use this tool with lower sums by investing in mutual funds which purchase Ginnie Maes. We will discuss mutual funds later in this book.

There are many other types of government issues from a variety of federal banks and agencies. However, the other issues are usually only bought and sold by the managers of large pools of money such as insurance companies and pension funds. The managers of these large sums of money are collectively known as *institutional investors* since they invest the money of their particular organizations or institutions. Some of the federal banks and agencies that you may hear of that offer these securities are Federal Home Loan Banks, Federal Land Banks, or possibly the Federal National Mortgage Association (nicknamed Fannie Mae).—Note—You may notice listings of Fannie Mae common stock or debentures. This agency is set up as a standard corporation and, therefore, also offers these other money raising tools; however, these Fannie Mae stocks and bonds are *not* direct obligations of the federal government even though this is a federally set up organization. This corporation must stand on its own merit. If specific questions arise about these other government issues, it is best to consult your broker or tax advisor.

Now you have a good familiarity with the government-backed wealth building tools available—savings bonds, treasury bonds, and notes. Each offers an extremely safe type of investment at a variety of interest rates. Some offer a tax deferral feature (EE bonds). And some, such as savings bonds, are not transferable. The Ginnie Mae has the unique feature of monthly payments.

General Bond Information

Except for the bonds issued by the U.S. Government, all bonds are rated to give you an idea about their safety. How sure can you be that the organization you are loaning your money to will repay you and meet all interest promises? Bond ratings will show you the answer. The most common scale for bond rating is used by *Standard and Poor's Corporation*. All other scales are similar.

Generally, there is no reason to buy bonds of less than BBB quality. Some municipals may be an exception, but go no lower than a B rating here.

STANDARD AND POOR'S BOND RATING SCALE

AAA   Highest Quality
AA   High Quality
A   Good Quality
BBB   Medium Grade
BB   Risky, but with some good features
B   Risky, but with some good features
CCC   Highly Risky
CC   Highly Risky
C   No interest being paid now
D   Lowest rating

Bond listings in newspapers require some explanation. You would see SCC's bond issue, from the example used in the corporate bond section, listed in your newspaper something like this:

BONDS   **CLOSING PRICE**
SCC 7s03   100

The company's abbreviated name (SCC) is followed by the interest rate (7s = 7% annual interest rate), and then the year of maturity is stated using only the last two digits (2003 = 03). The market price is quoted by omitting the last zero (100 = $1,000 per bond).

You now know a great deal about these stock and bond tools which can help you reach your money goals. The large number of tools may seem to be a bit confusing and/or complicated at first. Just remember that there is no need to try to memorize the features of these tools, just become familiar with them. This book will serve as a ready reference when questions arise. Also, try to put off the inevitable questions about choosing the best tool from the very many available tools. When we get to section three of this book, those questions will not seem as hard to answer as they might seem right now. For now let's try to become as familiar as possible with the tools that we can choose from. Later, we will use Part Three's wealth building guide to help you with your selections. Next, we will look at a much publicized area known as the "Money Market."

CHAPTER 6

Money Market Tools

In recent years, the "money market" has been the most talked about and written about method of pursuing money goals. And yet it seems that there is still a lot of misunderstanding about this marketplace. The publicity would suggest that money market opportunities are a fairly new development. In actuality, they have existed as long as most other money making opportunities. They had been spotlighted because they had been offering exceptionally high interest rates. Also, these money market tools were made accessible to the small investor through mutual funds and special bank accounts. Before this, minimum investments starting at $10,000 shut out a lot of small investors.

But exactly what is this "money market" so highly touted as being *the* place to put your money for highest current interest rates? How does it work? Does it have something to offer to everyone? These and other mysteries can be solved as we look at the parts of the money market and learn about their advantages and disadvantages.

The term **money market** is actually the name of one of the two markets used for investments. The other market is called the capital market. Investors can invest in either the money market or the capital market or some combination of the two. Organizations can obtain needed money from either the money market or the capital market. The choice must be one or the other or some combination of the two; nothing else exists. The **capital market** is the one we have been discussing up to this point. It contains all the money tools designed for the long term (more than one year), i.e., all the stock and bond tools. The money market contains the short term (less than one year) money tools which are used by most of the same people who use the capital market. Let's return now to Smart Computers Corporation to learn about one of these money market tools—commercial paper.

Commercial Paper

Smart Computers Corporation (SCC) found that from time to time it needed to have access to large chunks of money for only a short time. Occasionally, these chunks were even larger than SCC's bank wanted to loan. When this occurred, SCC would turn to investors for the needed money and would issue an I.O.U. This type of I.O.U. is called **commercial paper** and represents a debt of the company. When investors buy commercial paper, they are actually loaning their money to the company similar to bond purchases. Commercial paper is sold with face values ranging from $100,000 to $1,000,000 and has a life (or term) of up to 270 days. These issues are initially sold at discount (like savings bonds) which means you would pay less than the face amount and receive the exact face amount at the end of the term. The discounted purchase price is calculated to reflect the amount you will receive as interest at term's end. The amount of interest paid to investors in commercial paper is usually the highest paid on any money market tool.

SCC found that to be sure of raising the needed sums of money in the money market it had to offer an interest of 10%. This meant that for every $100 they received, they had to promise to pay back $105 at the end of the issue's 180-day term (10% of $100 = $10, but payable for only ½ year = $5 interest). SCC found that because of the large face amounts of commercial paper (minimum $100,000) the investors almost always would be mutual funds, pension funds, other corporations, or banks.

SCC was not the only organization needing cash for a short period. Banks are continuously searching for money to supply their lending operations. Frequently, they will issue money market tools called certificates of deposit.

Certificates of Deposit

Banks issue **certificates of deposit** to raise money for their short-term operations. These issues, known as CDs for short, sell at face value. CDs are usually sold in bearer form (whoever holds the paper can redeem them; they are not registered in any name), and they obligate the bank to repay the principal (face value) plus interest. The minimum purchase has recently been reduced. The most common minimum is now $2,500, but some banks offer CDs at even lower amounts. Thus, even the small investor can use this money tool.

There is a substantial penalty if the money is withdrawn before the CD maturity date. For example, if you buy a 6-month, $5,000 CD at 10% interest and have to withdraw your money after only 3 months, you would sacrifice all of the 3 months' interest. Since the 10% interest rate is based on one year, the math would look like this: ($5,000 × 10% = $500 interest, but only for ½ year = $250 interest; after three months, interest = $125 −3 months $125 penalty = $0 interest.) If you left your money in less than the penalty period (in this case, 3 months), you would lose some of the original invested amount (principal). If you withdrew after only one month, you would receive only $4,916.67. (Earned interest after one month = $41.67 −$125 penalty = −$83.34; $5,000 −$83.34 = $4,916.67.)

These CDs are issued with terms ranging from a few days to one year and are very safe investments. No loss, other than penalty, has ever been recorded on a CD investment. CDs are a good place to "park" idle money not needed for a short time. The interest they pay is taxable as simple income to the holder. We will talk more about CDs when we cover banks and savings and loans. Let's look now at another money market tool used by banks.

Bankers' Acceptances

Another money market tool used by banks is called **bankers' acceptances.** Because they are sold in $100,000 minimums, smaller investors need to know about them only because many mutual funds, pension funds, or insurance companies invest in them. Banks use them to finance deals in certain products or to enable import/export deals in connection with foreign banks. They are sold at discount, and maturities can be as long as 270 days.

Treasury Bills (T-Bills)

Just like banks and corporations, the federal government also needs cash for short periods. **Treasury bills** are short-term government issues that have maturities of three months to one year. When the government sells these, it is operating in the money market.

Treasury bills are extremely safe investments like treasury notes and bonds. The "full faith and credit" of the federal government is behind them. They are sold at discount from face value. In other words, the interest to be paid on them is subtracted (discounted) from the amount you pay for them. At maturity, they are redeemed at full face value. Because treasury bills are so safe, they usually pay less interest than other money market tools. When discussing T-bills, they are referred to by their yield—for example, 8% T-bills. The minimum face value of T-bills is $1,000, and the interest income is taxable at the federal level only.

Commercial paper, CDs, bankers' acceptances, and T-bills are the tools available for use in the money market. All these issues are for the short term of less than one year. Interest rates will be the highest for commercial paper and the lowest for T-bills. T-bills have the highest degree of safety and commercial paper the lowest. Investors can use these tools directly, or they can use them indirectly by investing in mutual funds or special banking accounts.

The term money market is simply the name of the market where these short term issues are bought and sold. Both the capital and money markets are not actual places but rather they are the names given to categories of money tools. The money market has existed for a long time, but very attractive interest rates spotlighted it and caused its popularity to explode. Let's turn now to a common method of using money market and capital market tools—a device that enables the small investor to have access to all money tools—mutual funds.

CHAPTER 7

Mutual Funds

Mutual funds have a very good chance of being the right tool for some parts of your wealth building project. They are a very important consideration, no matter what your personal situation. Well over $250 Billion (and, that's Billion with a "B") is currently invested in mutual funds. Countless millions of Americans are using this tool to pursue their money objectives. Mutual funds are a well-used tool in both the capital market and, of course, the money market. These funds are designed with the small investor's needs in mind. They are affordable, professionally managed, lower risk tools that offer the small investor the opportunities that otherwise would be out of reach.

Is this one of the right tools for reaching your money goals? Is there a fund tailored to meet your particular needs? How do these funds work? Are there any basic differences you need to be aware of? All these are important questions. They require answers if you are to make wise decisions about using this tool instead of, or in addition to, other tools. The logical way to start our examination of this money tool is by determining exactly what a basic mutual fund is.

Mutual Fund Basics

Mutual Fund is a word coined to describe a type of investment company. The sum of money invested (the fund) in these companies will be managed for maximum gain, and all investors will mutually share, hence the name Mutual Fund. In other words, a mutual fund collects a large number of small investments into a pool. This pooled money is then reinvested by professional money managers. All gains (or losses) from these reinvestments are then passed back to the original investor.

A mutual fund company, similar to any other corporation, offers shares of its common stock for sale. This is the way it acquires the pool of money it will then reinvest. When you buy the shares of a mutual fund, you actually own a piece of it. You are then an owner and not a lender.

The mutual fund's reason for existence is the professional management of your invested money. That is its main objective and must not be (by law) only a sideline. Bank and insurance companies also invest large pools of money, but they do not qualify as mutual funds. Their investment activity is not their main business. To maintain their tax-free status, mutual fund companies pay strict attention to investments and are careful not to dabble in other non-related activities. This is to *your* benefit as an investor because you can be sure the company is concentrating on one thing—trying to make the best possible investment decisions for your money.

The terms, **open-end** and **closed-end,** are used to separate two types of investments—mutual funds and investment companies. The whole money pooling concept started with investment companies. They operate exactly like standard corporations and are closed-end, i.e., once they have sold their initial issue of stock, they have no further direct buying or selling contact with their investors. Mutual funds, on the other hand, create and sell new shares on a continuous basis, and they buy back the shares their investors want to sell. The number of shares fluctuates and is unlimited, thus they have an open-end.

All open-end mutual funds will either be load funds or no-load funds. They operate exactly alike in every way except one. The **load funds** charge a sales commission (a "load") when you buy their shares; the **no-load funds** do not. This load or sales charge is subtracted from the invested amount. For instance, if you paid $1,000 into a fund, you may receive only $915 worth of its shares with $85 subtracted for the sales fee. If you decide upon a no-load fund, the entire $1,000 would be invested because there is no sales fee. It should be noted, however, that some no-load funds charge a fee—usually one or two percent—when you sell back your shares.

Why would anyone purchase a load fund and pay the sales charge when he can purchase shares of a no-load fund at no charge? There is no clear-cut answer to this question. For instance, the answer is not in fund quality. There are funds of both load and no-load types that have made substantial gains for their investors. Simply because a fund charges a sales commission does not mean that its managers are any better or worse than the managers of no-load funds. Some funds have done very well at producing gains and some have not, regardless of load or no-load type.

Load funds have sales people who will call on you. Some say these sales people are *the* big advantage of load funds. In essence, they say, you are hiring a personal investment advisor to help you with investment decisions. The salesperson can explain all about fund provisions and how they work and can answer all your questions before you decide. After the sale he would be available if any problems or further questions arise. This is all true. However, you must keep in mind that the driving force behind every salesperson is the sale—specifically, the sale of his particular fund. No sale—no pay. Therefore, if you have poor sales resistance, the salesperson is a good reason to avoid load funds. You could end up with a fund not matched to your needs, or you could end up with a poorly performing fund. Good sales resistance? Then the salesperson could be a good source of information.

The final deciding factor in selecting the fund should not be based on whether it is load or no-load but should rest on one main question: How well has the fund done its job of producing gains for its investors? Compare it with other like mutual funds.

Mutual Fund Advantages

When you buy ownership shares in a mutual fund, in effect, you contract or delegate investment decisions to someone else. In fact, this **professional management** is a major advantage of mutual funds. By using this tool, an inexperienced investor can use the expert services of full-time money managers. These professional managers will make all necessary decisions about the fund's investments—when and what to sell, buy, or hold. Of course, some of these fund managers are very good and some are not. But most funds, especially the leading ones, are managed by sharp, high caliber managers with large amounts of investment experience.

Another major advantage offered by mutual funds is **diversification.** For the small investor, this is a very good way to heed an old warning about not putting all your eggs in one basket. A mutual fund invests in a great many different companies and industries. Because of this, if one investment turns bad, the effect on the overall fund is minimized. You, as a shareholder, own a small portion of each of the many investments of the fund. The impact on you will also be minimized because of this broad spread of different investments. For example, if you bought the stock of ABC Company and the company went under, you would lose 100% of your investment. Now, let's say you put that same money into a mutual fund which owned the same ABC stock along with, say, 49 other companies' stock. If ABC went under now, your loss would only be 1/50th or 2% of your invested money. This is a greatly simplified example, but the concept will hold true. These funds, as a rule, will not invest more than 5% in any one company.

The **ease of record keeping** for a mutual fund investment is another advantage. The fund keeps a record of prices and dates, tallies up all transactions, and reports the year-end results to you in time for tax reports. Its day-to-day performance can be tracked as easily as opening the newspaper.

MUTUAL FUND ADVANTAGES

Professional Management—Lets the pros make the decisions.

Diversification—Minimizes your risk.

Easy Record Keeping—They keep the records.

ADVANTAGES YOU MAY CHOOSE TO USE

Most mutual funds offer an **automatic reinvestment** choice. If you ask these companies, they will take your earnings and automatically buy additional shares. This would be a good idea for those not needing the earnings for current living expenses.

Another attractive provision would be an **exchange privilege.** Many mutual funds are a part of a family of mutual funds with each designed for a different purpose. Some may be designed to provide you with current income; others may provide long-term growth. These fund families usually offer an exchange privilege. This makes it possible to switch your investment from one fund to another, without cost, within certain limits. This is an important advantage as your investment goals change.

Another advantage offered by some funds are various forms of **accumulation plans.** These plans are a very good idea for the person who just never gets around to saving the money he knows he is going to need later. Similar to payroll savings plans, they are a means of "forced savings." These plans also serve those who are starting their wealth building program from zero. The minimum investment to start these plans is generally only $50. In essence, these plans are legal contracts between you and the fund.

ADVANTAGES YOU MAY CHOOSE TO USE

Automatic Reinvestment—Your profits would buy more fund shares.

Exchange Privilege—You may switch between funds.

Accumulation Plans—You may make a savings contract.

ACCUMULATION PLAN TYPES

There are three basic types of accumulation plans. The first type is called a **voluntary accumulation plan** and is the most flexible. It allows you to invest (buy mutual fund shares) any amount you want, whenever it is convenient for you. It is simply a written promise by you to make future purchases. A second type of accumulation plan is called a **periodic payment plan.** This is a more rigid contract, and you promise to invest a set amount of money at specific intervals for a fixed period of time. For example, you may agree to invest $25 a month for five years (you set the terms).

The third and last type of accumulative plan is called a **variable annuity** and is a type of retirement plan. It works like this: You agree to pay in or invest a certain amount, either in a lump sum or over a period of time. The company would then invest your money and at a specific time, usually your retirement, the company agrees to pay back your invested money and any earnings at regular intervals. The amount that you will receive will depend on how profitable the investments were. Thus, the amounts you receive can vary, and hence, the name variable annuity.

The first two types of plans are referred to as **front-end-load plans.** This term describes *when* the sales commission or load is collected—during the first payments at the front end of the plan. This means the sales charge for the entire plan will be deducted from your first payments with only a portion of your money going to actual investments. Some plans claim to minimize this by offering a **spread load plan;** however, these basically are still a front-end-load type with initial sales charge deductions only slightly lower than other plans.

ACCUMULATION PLANS
(CONTRACTED SAVINGS PLANS)

Voluntary Accumulation*—No set amount or time of payments.

Periodic Payment Plan*—Definite amounts and times for payments.

Variable Annuities—Pay-ins by lump sum or spread out. Pay-outs are for as long as you live.

---

*Front-end-load plans—total plan commissions are deducted from the first payments.

All three of these plans have important rules and regulations that must be understood. For instance, most of these plans charge a hefty penalty if the plan is stopped before the contract is fulfilled. It is essential that you completely understand all the terms of the contract before you sign anything.

These accumulation plans may be just the tool you need in the construction of your wealth building program, but, please, take the time and ask the necessary questions to be sure you know what you are doing.

VALUE MEASUREMENT

Previously, we discussed the various values of stocks and bonds. Unlike those, mutual funds have only one value as quoted in the media—**Net Asset Value (NAV)**. This is the amount you will receive when you sell your shares and pay when you buy (+ any load). The Net Asset Value of mutual fund stock is figured by adding up everything the company owns and dividing this sum by the number of shares. For example, if everything the fund owned had a combined value of $5 million and there were one million shares, the NAV per share would be $5.00. This is the value quoted as the bid price and is the amount you receive if you sell your shares back to the company. The offer price is quoted alongside the bid price and is the amount you have to pay to buy the stock. The offer price will be higher than the bid price (NAV) to reflect any load (sales charges). No-load funds, therefore, have the same bid and offer prices. Mutual fund shares generally have NAV's in the $5–$10 range.

Money Market Funds

Some mutual funds, as indicated earlier, specialize in just one area. Those which reinvest your money in the tools of the *short term money market* are known by the name of their specialty—**money market funds.** The interest earned by these funds from the money market is passed through to shareholders. These funds offer a big advantage to smaller investors. These smaller investors would not otherwise have access to most of these money market tools. If you recall, most money market tools have very high minimum investment requirements. These high minimums shut out the little guy. Money market funds let him in.

The money market fund is a fairly recent development. The first ones appeared in 1974. In 1979, these funds rapidly gained popularity. The reason for their popularity was the fact that they offered a 10% return, checking privileges, and could be so easily obtained by answering ads in newspapers and magazines or by contacting stockbrokers. Those who then filled out the paperwork and mailed in a check were feeling really good about doubling the rate they had been getting at their bank. Then, in 1981, when interest rates went skyrocketing, their popularity did, too. At their peak, more than 12 million people had invested over $250 billion in these money market funds. The interest rate paid by these funds has now decreased, and is expected to remain at a respectable but comparatively unimpressive 7–9%. (At their peak these funds paid as much as 18%.) Thus, their popularity has decreased and many investors have withdrawn in favor of other investments.

These original money market funds now very closely resemble banking accounts. This is by design. To attract and keep investors interested, these funds are offering more and more services. Most offer checking and some offer unlimited checking. Also, a large number offer nationally honored credit card services. Since these funds now compete with banks, some even offer insurance to guarantee the value of their shares. All these privileges and services have a cost, sometimes stated as a fee and other times accounted for by withholding a small portion of the earned interest.

Unlike any other mutual funds, all money market fund shares have a net asset value (NAV) of $1.00 per share. If you invest $500, you will receive 500 shares. The media will list different money market funds by quoting each yield, i.e., ABC fund may be paying 8.5% and DEF fund may pay 7.9%. This yield is actually the earnings, or interest, you will receive if you own some of the fund. The yield you receive may change daily; however, you can keep track of this changeable yield in most newspapers.

Many of the larger stock brokers offer money market funds in combination with their other services. These combination accounts provide an automatic parking place for idle investment monies and make these sums readily available for some future need. The account would work like this: Let's say you owned shares of stock in companies A, B, and C and were keeping $1,000 for a known upcoming expense. This account would provide you with a monthly report recording the status of your stock and the earnings of your $1,000 in the money market fund. If you request it, all earnings from the fund and any dividends from your stock will automatically be reinvested in more shares of the money market fund. They will immediately begin earning interest. When you sell some or all of your stock in one of the companies (A, B, or C), these proceeds also would then be immediately invested in the fund and begin earning interest. When another company's stock is purchased, the amount needed would automatically be taken from the money fund share account.

This combination account also provides checking services with an important advantage. For instance, if you wrote a check against the $1,000 in the above example, the $1,000 would continue to earn daily interest until the check cleared. The time between writing the check and clearing the check can sometimes be as long as 7 days. The same concept applies to credit card use. Charge a purchase using the fund's credit card, and you continue to earn interest until the charge is paid. So, you see, this one account provides all these services and gives you a monthly statement recording all activity. Again, these services are not without cost. The amount charged will be in the form of either a straight fee (yearly) or a portion of the money market fund's earnings or some combination of both. This type of account is an attractive hassle-free method of tracking your wealth building activity.

Other Mutual Fund Types

The variety of available mutual funds is limited only by your imagination. Almost every imaginable method of pursuing money goals will have a mutual fund type designed especially for it. These funds differ only in the selection of the tools they will use to produce the hoped for gains. Some funds will invest only in one type of money tool. For example, a bond fund would invest only in bonds, and an even more specialized fund may invest only in a certain type of bonds such as Government bonds.

There are income funds and growth funds. There are combination funds, sometimes known as balanced funds, which invest in some combination (a balance) of stocks and bonds for income or growth. Some stock funds choose only well established, proven (blue chip) stock, and others will concentrate on new, promising, but more risky, stock. There are some funds which only buy the Ginnie Mae issues we talked about in the bond section, and others are composed entirely of tax-free municipal bonds. There is even one fund which invests only in the stocks which make up the Dow Jones Industrial Average. The Dow Jones Average is the one you hear quoted everyday in the news. Therefore, when you buy this fund, you buy the Dow Average, and changes in your fund value will be exactly the same as changes in the Dow Jones Industrial Average. There are also funds that invest solely in other funds.

So, you see, the variety of mutual fund types can fulfill just about any need. A recent issue of the *Wall Street Journal* listed 550 individual mutual funds. Some were similar, but all had different management or purposes. There is a good chance that one or more of these mutual funds may be for you.

You may hear of a close relative of the mutual fund—**unit investment trusts.** These trusts do not issue common stock like a mutual fund, but rather, they issue certificates called Shares (or units) of Beneficial Interest (SBI). Unlike a mutual fund, a unit investment trust requires only a minimum amount of management and, therefore, has minimum management costs. The trust will buy a collection of different bonds and then sell pieces of the collection (SBIs) to investors. From then on the collection can not change (no further trading). The number of available SBIs is fixed; the cost is $1,000. Each SBI represents a partial ownership of each bond in the collection. Investors usually receive interest in the form of monthly interest checks. Municipal bonds are a popular investment for these unit investment trusts.

In summary, we have heard about many aspects of this money tool called a mutual fund. We have heard about those funds with open and closed ends and those with and without loads. We saw how their shares are valued, and read about some mutual fund advantages. These funds come in all shapes, sizes, and varieties with the current most popular variety being the money market fund. It is important to remember that all of the services, advantages, provisions, and features of mutual funds do not come without cost. There may be sales fees (load) when you buy, or redemption fees when you sell. There will be management fees which come from fund profits. Mutual funds may be a very wise selection for your particular wealth building program. These funds do offer the means by which even the "little guy" can use some of the more expensive money tools. The mutual funds do not offer a way to get rich quick; however, their advantages do merit your consideration. Let us turn next to something almost everyone is interested in: The Banking World.

CHAPTER 8

Banks

SEARS, ROEBUCK & CO.?!?!?

First, a word about a word—Banks. At one time, there was a distinct difference between banks, savings and loans, credit unions, etc. In the wake of the revolution described below these differences have all but disappeared. Banks may still have the different names, but the services they provide you, their customer, are the same. The different names only serve to point out the different ways in which these establishments were originally organized. Herein we are only concerned with the services available to you in your pursuit of money goals. Therefore, throughout this text, the word banks will be used to describe all these types of establishments.

The Banking Revolution

"Happenings" in the banking world have been occurring at a rapid rate. Recent changes in banking have come fast and furious. Now that most of the dust has settled, it can be seen that these changes were nothing short of revolutionary. Until just a few years ago, when you walked into a bank your expectations and choices were simple. You could open a checking account or a passbook savings account. Money in the savings account would earn 5¼% or 5½% just as it had for at least the last 50 years. Banks were thought of in such terms as safe, stable, predictable, unchanging, or sure. If you needed your money, you simply took it out of the bank without the remotest thought of any consequences of the withdrawal.

All this has changed now. Banks now offer many different ways and means of depositing your money and many forms of checking accounts for your use. The choice between the options is complicated and compounded by a host of different interest rates, terms, penalties, and a lot of good old-fashioned hoop-la. Banks now offer interest rates ranging from the standard 5¼% to as high as 25%. Bank accounts are now known by names like Premium, NOW, or even Super NOW. Banks also now toss around another new term, a mysterious thing called a penalty. Now, for the first time, if you withdraw too much of your money or take it out too soon, you may have to "pay a penalty." It could be that you would even *lose* part of the money you put in! How can this be? What's going on?

This chapter will sort out all the "goings on" in the world of banking. Hopefully, by the end of this chapter, you will be able to recognize the differences in the new tools now offered by banks and will know what to "look for" and what to "look out for."

From Stability to Change

BANKING AT SEARS?!?!

What could cause such sweeping, far-ranging changes in the banking world? Part of the cause can be explained with one word—deregulation. Federal and State rules and regulations have kept banks stable and assured everyone of a safe, dependable, and unchanging place to go for money services. Savings and Loan Associations offered their specialty— savings accounts and home loans. The smaller Credit Unions served their special interest groups with savings accounts and small loans. Commercial banks served everyone's needs for checking accounts, passbook savings accounts, and all varieties of loans. Each type of bank had rules and regulations to govern its operations and to protect each type of bank from the excessive competition of other types. They were told how much interest they could pay and what services and/or options they could offer. Recently, however, many of these rules and regulations have been drastically reduced or eliminated.

The recent deregulation of the banking business has brought about the many changes we are witnessing. It is now very difficult to tell the difference between bank types. Now, all offer checking, savings, and loan services, and all are engaged in fierce competition for your business. Full-page newspaper and magazine ads and repeated TV and radio commercials attempt to lure you to their new, one-stop service operation.

What caused banks to react so swiftly and drastically to deregulation? To understand this, we must look at the happenings in another area—mutual funds. The last chapter on mutual funds outlined the recent history of a specialized type of fund called a money market fund. When it first appeared in 1974, no one, including the banks, hardly noticed it. When money market interest rates went through the roof in 1979 and 1980, people deserted the banks in droves. It was hard for the banks not to notice the disappearance of $250,000,000,000 (billion) from their accounts. Because of Federal and State rules and regulations, the banks could not compete with these new money market funds. If banks were going to survive as a viable alternative, the laws had to change. And change they did.

The United States Congress formed the Depository Institutions Deregulation Committee. This committee, which had such notable members as the Secretary of the Treasury and the Chairman of the Federal Reserve, was given the task of changing the rules that had kept banks from being competitive. They raised ceilings and lowered floors: Interest rate ceilings were removed, and minimum deposits were lowered from limits that used to range from $7,000 to $20,000 to a more reasonable $2,500. And, now, the competition is intense!

The competition for money fund investors has caused fast and furious changes in banking. Both banks and funds offer high interest on check writing services and savings accounts. The differences between banks and funds have grown smaller and smaller, and differences between types of banks have all but disappeared. Some funds, to compete with banks which flount federally insured accounts, have formed some strange alliances. One fund, run by Dean Witter Reynolds, invests shareholders' monies in the new money market accounts of Allstate Savings and Loan; thus, they can claim the same type of federally insured accounts as banks. And, who owns and houses the stock brokerage of Dean Witter Reynolds and the Allstate Savings and Loan? Sears Roebuck, of course. Banking at Sears—you can today! Can a J.C. Penney checking account be far behind? Deregulation enabled competition that made it happen.

Banks first offered money market savings accounts in December, 1982. To attract new customers, they paid exceptionally high interest rates on these accounts; one bank offered 25% interest to new savers, and many other bank rates hovered around 20%. Money market mutual funds could offer only 7–9%, and, therefore, the stampede was on to the banks. Hundreds of thousands of new depositors swarmed into bank lobbies across the nation. Some smaller branch offices looked like theatres on premiere night with lines formed out the door and into the parking lot. Depositors were filling out paperwork on each other's backs, in their laps, and on the floor.

By January, 1983, one month later, the stampede had slowed and bank rates for savings accounts were now in the 10–12% range. Banks now offered interest-bearing checking accounts with interest rates based on money market rates, and they had put the new $2,500 minimum for Certificates of Deposit into effect. The dust had pretty well settled by the end of January and the success of the new offerings was obvious. Banks were thriving. Money market mutual fund investments had decreased from $250 billion to $200 billion in only 60 days.

Banks now found it impossible to continue to offer artificially high interest rates. Banks generally have a high overhead cost stemming from elaborate buildings and large staffs, so they could now only offer savings account interest rates equal to or slightly lower than rates paid by leading money market funds. The new checking accounts are very expensive for the banks. To run a checking account for one year usually costs $95 plus approximately 40¢ for processing each check.

These expenses result in a lower interest rate for checking accounts.

Banking Pros and Cons

One of the advantages of using banks is *safety*. This safety factor is used heavily in advertising campaigns designed to lure new depositors. Your deposited money would be "safe" with them because all deposits are "federally insured." This insurance protection originated in the 1930s after so many banks had failed, and depositors had lost everything. The U.S. Congress set up two separate insurance corporations to protect depositors in the event of any future bank failures. Your bank deposits, whether in a Commercial bank, Savings and Loan, or Credit Union, are protected by either the FDIC (Federal Deposit Insurance Corporation) or the FSLIC (Federal Savings and Loan Insurance Corporation). There is no significant difference between these two insurance companies, and both insure any deposited amount up to $100,000, regardless of whether you use a checking account, savings account, withdrawable shares, investment certificates, or just plain deposits. If you have more than $100,000 deposited, and the bank fails, you would have to wait until all possessions of the bank were sold and all bills were paid; should any money be left, you will receive your additional sums.

This insurance was put to the test in 1982 when well over 40 banks failed. These failures were, at least in part, caused by the rush to the money market mutual funds. Now that banks can offer interest rates similar to money market fund rates, the high number of bank failures, mergers, and take-overs witnessed in 1982 (Did your local banks change names?) should not be seen again. Through all of those "bad times for banks" no one lost any part of deposited sums under $100,000, and most of those with more than $100,000 deposited received their additional sums, also.

Another feature of banking tools is *convenience*. Banks have made every attempt to assure you that there is a branch office "just around the corner." You can use your banking card to withdraw money at these branch offices at any time. You can just "drop in" on your way to or from work or the market.

Banks have done a good job of making their services convenient and accessible to you, their customer.

Another aspect of using banks as a wealth building tool is a difficult one to explain, but strong, *emotional factor*. Many people strongly prefer to turn over their money to the "friendly teller" at the bank "just around the corner" rather than try to find a broker or to mail their money to an address "half across the country." This personal contact offered by banks gives many a feeling of confidence. Emotional factors can affect bankers, too. Just the fact that the banker knows you, can make it easier to get a loan.

This has been the good news; now, for some bad news. There are some features that can cause unexpected injury to your wealth building program. Be very cautious of bank penalties; these penalties can be in many forms and sizes. There may be a penalty for withdrawing your deposited money too soon or for withdrawing too much of your money. *You may even pay a penalty for doing nothing.* For example, you may deposit a small sum in a bank account in your child's name to teach him about saving or banking. Then, for any number of reasons, you do not make any deposits or withdrawals to this account for some time. When the child does finally withdraw the money, there may be less than you put in! Banks can charge a fee for inactive accounts. In fact, since banks take money from the account itself for payment of the fees, if small sums were left inactive long enough, the entire amount would be lost to fees.

Checking services may be free as long as a certain amount is left in the account. If the account balance falls below this minimum amount, penalty fees would be charged. Savings accounts may pay a high interest rate as long as the account contains at least a certain amount; any less and a penalty is imposed by drastically reducing the interest. The penalty imposed on Certificates of Deposit (CDs) for early withdrawals can be particularly severe. If, for some reason, you asked for the money you had deposited in a CD before the maturity date, you could lose part or all of the interest payable to you. It is conceivable that you may even lose part of the amount originally deposited. For instance, if you needed to withdraw the money from a six month CD after only two months, the penalty would be three months' worth of interest. Since you have earned only two months' worth, the rest would be subtracted from the amount you originally paid into the CD.

The penalties and fees are already plentiful at banks, and they will probably increase in both number and size. As mentioned earlier, running a bank is expensive. If banks are going to remain competitive with the money funds, they must offer high interest, yet cover operating costs and remain profitable. To do this, they probably will increase costs to customers. Watch for increased costs in such areas as charges for writing more than a maximum number of checks, making more than a maximum number of deposits during a certain period, and charges per check. Let's look at specific bank tools that have become available since the banking revolution.

Types of Bank Accounts

There are two basic ways that a bank can deal with the money you give them, i.e., in a regular checking account or a standard savings account. Most banks now offer a banking card service in conjunction with checking accounts. This card looks exactly like a credit card and can be used to withdraw cash from your account anytime, day or night, seven days a week, at machines in convenient locations. A familiar type of savings account is referred to as a Passbook Account. When making deposit or withdrawal in this account, you pass a small account book to the bank teller, then, after recording the activity in the book, the teller passes the book back to you. Hence, the name. Not all banks use such a book. Many simply give a receipt for your deposit, and withdrawals can be made by simply showing proper identification. There is no minimum amount required by law to start one of these accounts; however, most banks do specify a $5.00 minimum.

NOW ACCOUNTS

Banks somehow needed to compete with the checking accounts offered by money market mutual funds. Your money, when invested in a money fund, would earn high interest rates, and, yet, you could write a check against it at anytime. To compete, the banks designed a system that enabled them to also pay interest on a checking account. This special checking account is called **NOW checking**—the name stands for *Negotiated Order of Withdrawal*—and, it is a combination savings and checking account. When you make a deposit in a NOW account, the money is put in the savings side of this account and will earn 5¼% interest. When writing a check using a NOW account, you, in the bank's terms, are actually negotiating a special order to the bank to make a withdrawal (Negotiated Order of Withdrawal) from your savings. In other words, banks can now pay interest on checking accounts by referring to the checks by other terms and by changes in their accounting systems. You, the customer, use a NOW checking account exactly like a regular checking account.

The law does not impose a minimum deposit for NOW accounts; however, banks generally require that you keep at least $1,000 in the account to avoid paying fees. If the account balance drops below the minimum figure, the bank may charge a monthly service charge of $5–$10 and/or 20–30¢ for every check.

When the banking laws changed during the first part of 1983, they allowed the banks to offer checking accounts paying high rates of interest closer to those paid by money funds. The banks call these checking accounts **Super NOW Accounts.** The basic workings of these newer accounts are the same as the older NOW accounts; however, the Super NOW have no maximum payable interest rate, and you must maintain a $2,500 minimum balance. Banks tie the interest amount to current rates in the money market. The interest paid on Super NOW checking accounts is variable but probably will remain higher than the 5¼% paid on NOW accounts. The Super NOW accounts were paying 6% to 8% in early 1983. Banks can guarantee a rate for as long as one month; however, most do not and refigure what they will pay on a daily basis. If your balance drops below $2,500, the bank can only pay you the 5¼% interest of a NOW account. In other words, when your Super NOW account balance is less than $2,500, the account reverts to the status of a NOW account. Because checking accounts are so expensive for the bank, interest rates payable on Super NOW checking accounts will be 1% to 3% lower than rates available on savings accounts (money market accounts) or money market funds.

MONEY MARKET SAVINGS ACCOUNTS

Before December of 1982, the only way a bank could offer savers interest rates comparable to money market funds was through certificates of deposit. There are so many strings attached to these CDs that they are really no competition for the relatively flexible money market funds. When the law changed in December of 1982, banks began offering the more competitive **Money Market Savings Account.** This new account basically works the same as a regular or passbook savings account. The important difference, of course, is the higher rate of interest it will pay. Banks now base their interest on the rates of the money market.

These bank money market accounts were paying extremely high rates in December of 1982 and January of 1983 to lure new depositors. The rates came down steadily then to a more comparable 8% to 9.5%. Banks can guarantee the rate for as long as one month; however, most banks refigure on a daily basis, with some guaranteeing rates for as long as one week. To obtain these variable but higher rates, the law requires that you keep at least $2,500 in the account. If the account balance drops below $2,500, the highest rate payable would then be 5½%, the same as a standard savings rate. These money market savings accounts will allow you to write checks against them up to a maximum of six withdrawals per month. Three checks can be payable to other persons/companies and three can be for cash. Banks advertise this checking provision to show that your money is obtainable at any time without penalty (unlike CDs). These accounts should not be thought of as checking accounts but rather, as savings accounts where your money is constantly and easily accessible. Remember, you must keep a $2,500 minimum in order to enjoy the higher rates.

NOTE: These new accounts may have a variety of names. Each bank will use names they believe will be more attractive than a competitor's. You will see names like Market Interest

BANK ACCOUNT COMPARISON

Type of Account	Legal Minimum	Common Minimum	Interest Rate	Penalties
Checking Regular	NONE	$5.00 (To open) $100–$500 (For cost free)	-0-	Fees charged if balance is less than minimum
NOW	NONE	$1,000	5¼%	Fees charged if balance is less than minimum
Super NOW	$2,500	$2,500	Variable, based on money market rates, 6%–7% common now	Interest drops to 5¼% if balance is less than minimum
Savings Passbook	NONE	$5.00 (To open)	5¼%–5½%	NONE (Except for inactive accounts charge)

BANK ACCOUNT COMPARISON *(Continued)*

Type of Account	Legal Minimum	Common Minimum	Interest Rate	Penalties
Savings Money Market	$2,500	$2,500	Variable, based on money market rates, 8%–10% common now	Interest drops to 5¼% if balance is less than minimum
CDs 7–91 Day Maturity	$2,500	$2,500	Fixed at time of deposit, based on money market rates, 7.5%–10% common now	Loss of all interest for early withdrawal
6 Month Maturity	$2,500	$2,500	Fixed at time of deposit, based on money market rates, 7.5%–10% common now	Loss of 3 months' interest for early withdrawal

Account, or Premium Account, or Super Interest Accounts. Regardless of the name, these accounts will all operate in the manner just described above.

We have reviewed the recent revolutionary happenings in the world of banking and have explored the reasons behind these happenings. You now know that you may see more seemingly strange developments due to deregulation and strong competition for your dollars. You now can "bank at Sears" or through a money market fund, or you can buy stocks at your local bank. Differences between types of banks (Commercial, Savings and Loans, Thrifts, Credit Unions) have all but disappeared, and they all offer several types of bank accounts such as the new money market savings accounts and the Super NOW checking accounts. The chart on the two previous pages will help you sort out, at a glance, the differences in these accounts. Now that we have become familiar with these money tools, let's turn to some special tools that will help you avoid excessive taxation.

CHAPTER 9

Tax Shelters, Options, and Other Specialized Hybrid Tools

The Hybrid Tools

Tax shelters and the other items in this chapter are hybrid tools; that is, they are modifications of the basic tools we have previously discussed. These tools are specifically designed to solve special wealth building problems. Being able to use them is like knowing the difference between using a wrench and a ratchet to tighten a bolt—the wrench, like the basic money tools, will do the job; but in some cases, the ratchet, like hybrid tools, will do it faster, easier, and better.

This chapter will familiarize you with the names, uses, and general design of the hybrid tools. If you decide to use these tools, be sure to obtain expert guidance. Up-to-date information and good advice is available from accountants, brokers, and, for some tools, from bankers. These experts can provide the skills you need to properly use these tools. This chapter will give you enough information to ask questions intelligently when using these experts. Let's now become familiar with the special tool most talked about—the tax shelter.

Tax Shelters

This area is of interest to more and more people. So many seem to be earning more but enjoying it less. If you succeed in keeping your income equal to the rising cost-of-living, your tax burden will become heavier and heavier. For example, if your income increased 3.9% in 1982 (3.9% was the rate of inflation), you could afford the same items you bought in 1981, and your standard of living would be the same as 1981. Right? Wrong. The 3.9% increase in income means you pay taxes on that cost-of-living increase, so 1981 earnings + 3.9% − taxes on 3.9% means you are worse off than you were in 1981. In fact, in many cases, that cost-of-living raise puts you into a higher tax bracket, and then you're even worse off than before. This subtle increase is known as "bracket creep." Hopefully, those who govern will see the unfairness of this "bracket creep" and will revise the laws to conform to reality.

Changes in the tax laws have been many and frequent. Even as this is written, lawmakers are contemplating further changes all in the name of "reform." Therefore, the legal tax advantages of today may be gone tomorrow, or they may have been "reformed" into unrecognizable shapes. The shelters covered here appear to be the most durable and should survive in the long run. Regardless of specific changes, the general descriptions will hold true and enable you to choose the type best suited to your personal situation. Do seek expert help when you use these tax shelters.

First, let's look at some terms you need to understand. **Tax avoidance** and **tax evasion** are two such terms, and the difference must be understood. Evasion can lead to jail. Measures designed to *evade* paying taxes are illegal and must be shunned. The tools described here are designed to enable you to *avoid* paying taxes by using legal methods encouraged by the laws. Congress passed these laws to aid various parts of the American economy. For example, the profits made on stock trading are not taxed as heavily as regular income. The tax laws applicable to this capital market were designed to encourage long-term investments in industry to keep it strong. All tax avoidance measures are legal ways to keep you from paying more taxes than need be—and, you will have the government's blessing.

A **tax shelter** is a tax avoidance tool. To fully understand shelters, you must know the difference between before tax and after tax dollars. Shelters are concerned with before tax dollars. As we covered the other tools in this book, we were talking about after tax dollars. Stocks or bonds are bought with money on which taxes have already been paid. Tax shelter investments use money before the tax bite, and, therefore, are much more advantageous. To illustrate, suppose you were in the 50% tax bracket. This means that out of every dollar you earn, 50¢ goes to Uncle Sam. To purchase a dollar's worth of stock or bonds, you must earn two dollars. With tax shelters every dollar earned can be put right to work before the tax bite. In general, the higher your income tax bracket, the more desirable a tax shelter will be.

Two more terms you need to know are **tax-free** and **tax-deferred**. Tax-free means you will never have to pay any taxes on the money. Tax-deferred sums will be taxed, but at some future date, hopefully, when you're in a lower bracket. Thus, you are simply delaying the payment of taxes on tax-deferred sums. Some examples may help. Municipal bonds pay tax-free income—no federal income tax. Earnings on the IRA plans talked about next are tax-deferred, i.e., you will pay taxes on IRA earnings, but at a future date. When putting money into this shelter, you use pre-tax dollars and amounts earned by this tax sheltered money are tax-deferred. You will be taxed on all tax shelter monies, both the investment and earnings, when you take the money out. The advantage is in choosing the time when taxes will be paid. Through these shelters you do not pay taxes on current income invested or on earnings of the investment until a future time when you may be in a lower tax bracket. Limited partnerships may offer an added feature—some can "pass through" certain deductions (tax avoidance) which owners can use on their personal income tax return year after year.

IRAs and Keogh plans are tax shelters designed to provide individuals with money when they reach retirement age. These plans are the government's response to the growing number of elderly, too many of whom depend solely on small sums of money provided by Social Security. These plans encourage the setting aside of sums of money by working individuals and businesses to provide money needed later in life. They are tax sheltered retirement plans. Let's look first at IRAs.

INDIVIDUAL RETIREMENT ACCOUNTS (IRAs)

An **IRA** is a tax sheltered personal retirement program provided for in the tax laws. This program can be used by anyone who receives income for his work, whether he is an employee or self-employed. The provisions of the latest changes, applicable to the tax year 1982, enable you or any wage earner to participate even if you are already covered by a Keogh plan or any other qualified retirement pension program. Even a non-working spouse can participate. The IRA plan allows you to set aside an amount of your yearly earnings up to a specified maximum. For tax year 1982, this maximum was $2,000, or, if you include your non-working spouse, $2,250. These maximums may change over the years. Amounts contributed to IRAs may not exceed 100% of your earned income. This is a significant limitation if, for example, you have a low wage but a large amount of dividend income or perhaps have received an inheritance. IRA amounts may be subtracted from gross income on your federal and most state income tax returns. Depending on how you set up the IRA, your invested money will earn interest and/or dividends, and these earnings also are not currently taxable. At age 59½ you may begin to withdraw from your IRA, and you must begin withdrawals by age 70½. If you become disabled, you can withdraw at any age. When money is taken from IRAs, it is taxed as ordinary income; however, the lower tax brackets of retirement will make the bite less severe.

An IRA may be set up through your broker, banker, or insurance agent. In other words, you may choose to invest IRA sums in stocks, bonds, or mutual funds (through brokers); CDs or special savings accounts (through your banker); or in annuities offered by insurance companies. It is also permissable to have more than one IRA—you may have sums invested in any combination of the above areas—as long as total amounts invested in all do not exceed maximums. The deadline for opening and/or contributing to an IRA is your tax filing deadline, usually April 15.

There is also a provision which allows the transfer of funds between different IRAs or into IRAs from other pension plans. This transfer is referred to as a **roll-over.** Sums from one tax sheltered account may be rolled over to another without tax consequence.

Removal of money from IRAs before age 59½ without a disability will result in penalties which are quite severe. If this premature withdrawal is a possibility for you, I strongly urge you to consult with a tax expert to learn about the latest changes to the law and gain an understanding of the consequences.

KEOGH PLANS

Keogh plans, named for the congressman who introduced them, are a close cousin of IRA plans. The main difference is that Keogh is used by businesses and not individual wage earners. A self-employed business person can shelter a certain percentage (15%, now) of income up to a maximum amount ($7,500, now). Keogh requires that, if the business has them, employees must also be included. Under current law, each participating employee must have worked for the company at least 1,000 hours a year for three years.

All other aspects of Keogh plans are like IRAs. Monies invested and future earnings on investments are not currently taxed, and withdrawals carry the same requirements with similar penalties for early withdrawals. Investments can be in any of a number of areas with slightly more restrictions as to which types of stocks and bonds may be purchased. If Keogh plans sound good to you, details and the latest information can be learned from your tax accountant, broker, banker, or insurance agent.

LIMITED PARTNERSHIPS

This tax shelter has long been an effective tool. Recent law changes and large increases in the number of limited partnerships have made these tax shelters available to more people today than ever before. A **limited partnership** is simply a form of business. The business performed by these partnerships can be anything from real estate management to oil and gas exploration. These limited partnership businesses are divided into shares, and the shares are sold to investors. Most shares are sold for prices of $10,000 or higher; however, some of these limited partnership shares can be purchased for as little as $1,000. These shares can be bought with pre-tax dollars.

As an investor, your liability would be limited to the money you invest. In other words, you may lose all of your investment, but would not be responsible for losses beyond that amount. This liability is the first of two limits represented by the name *limited* partnership. The other limit represented by the name is your participation. All management decisions are made by the general manager, and this person is responsible for the day-to-day running of the business. Your participation would be *limited* to your share of tax benefits and profits. You, as an investor and limited partner, would provide the start-up money for the business and, in return, would be legally entitled to certain tax benefits and profits. Start-up costs and first-year expenses for these businesses are usually high, and, therefore, your tax write-offs would be equally substantial. The initial reason for investing in a limited partnership would be the first years of possible tax deductions; however, the hope is that the business will succeed, for you would also receive a portion of profits.

Not too long ago, investing in these limited partnerships often resulted in tax deductions two or three times as large as the invested amount. For example, in the past, a $10,000 investment may have resulted in $20,000 worth of tax deductions. The latest change in the laws now limit this first year's tax benefits to 100% of investment. This means that in any one year a $10,000 investment can result in no more than $10,000 worth of tax deductions.

Limited partnerships have varying degrees of risk. Some are very risky; some are not. It should be remembered, however, that you, as an investor, would not be risking the entire invested sum. Part of that sum would have been lost to taxes anyway. For example, if you are in the 50% tax bracket, you would only be risking the 50% of your investment that you would *not* have paid Uncle Sam; if you are in the 30% bracket, you risk the 70% you would *not* have paid in taxes.

Some common types of limited partnership businesses are oil and gas drilling ventures, equipment leasing operations, and real estate. The oil and gas exploration types are, as might be expected, the most risky but have the greatest potential profit. It seems to be getting harder and harder to find a productive well, but the ones found can provide extremely high profits. The risks involved in another common type, equipment leasing, vary depending on lease provisions and the type of equipment leased, i.e., computers, office equipment, airplanes, ships, etc. A more common type of limited partnerships is real estate.

Real estate is the most attractive type of limited partnership. If these ventures are properly managed by reputable firms, the risk is minimal and the rewards handsome. In general, they work like this: You, as an investor and limited partner, would put up the money to purchase real estate properties of various descriptions. The type of real estate to be purchased will vary from one partnership to another. Some may deal only in shopping centers and/or small industrial developments renting space to businesses. Others may specialize in property to be rented as residences, such as apartment complexes. The manager/general partner decides which properties to buy or sell and when. The manager will keep the properties rented, provide for upkeep, and handle all the day-to-day problems. In other words, the general partner does all the work, and you receive the benefits in the form of tax write-offs or profits. The tax benefits can be large and long-lasting. The properties owned by the partnership can produce depreciation expenses which last for many years. On the other hand, when properties are finally sold, they usually produce fine profits.

There are many other types of limited partnerships; these have been only the most common. When considering one of these tax shelters, consult a tax expert and deal with reputable organizations. The risk element is always present, but by taking the above precautions, it will certainly be minimized.

Options

Options are *not* tax shelters. **Options** are special money tools designed to provide different methods of profiting from the movement of stock prices. They are included here and not in the chapter on stocks because they require an in-depth knowledge of stock trading and should be used only after careful study and with the assistance of a knowledgeable broker. You need to know they exist, their general description, and some terminology. The information provided here can be used as a starting point from which you can proceed to more in-depth studies. Whole books have been written on just this one tool—options.

The word option can be thought of as meaning opportunity. When the options are traded, investors are buying and selling the *opportunity* to buy and sell stock. For instance, a stockowner may sell the option (opportunity) of buying his stock. There are two types of options: puts and calls. Let's look at them one at a time.

CALLS

The term **call** is applied to these options because investors are actually buying the right to *call away* stock from its owner. More specifically, a call is the written right to purchase 100 shares of a named stock at a certain price before a specified date. Let's take SCC (Smart Computers Corporation) stock as an example. An SCC call might be written that offered 100 shares of SCC common stock at $40 a share if purchased anytime during the next three months. SCC is now selling at $39 a share. Investors may expect the price of SCC stock to increase *well above* $40 a share within three months. They would buy the call to profit from the expected SCC stock price increase without actually owning the stock. In the example above, a call might sell for $100 and the cost of buying the stock would be $3,900. Obviously, the amount of money at risk is not as much with a call as with outright stock ownership.

Many of those who invest in calls never buy the underlying stock. They simply resell the call before the expiration date to someone who actually wants to own the stock. In the example above, suppose SCC common increased to $43 a share within two months after the call was sold. The owner of the call now has the right to buy 100 shares of stock now selling for $43 for only $40 a share. The owner of the call would probably resell his right, now worth approximately $300, to someone wanting to own SCC stock. The call investor has thus tripled his money. The other side of the coin would be if the SCC stock price did not go up far enough or fast enough. If this happened, the call owner would lose the entire investment on the expiration date. Therefore, with calls, you can make nice profits or you can lose the whole investment if the underlying stock does not behave the way you expect. This, of course, is a greatly simplified example; in reality, an investor would probably buy ten SCC calls or more. The general principle holds true regardless of the simplification.

For every buyer there must be a seller; the seller of options is the person who writes up the offer and is called the writer. Writers sell options on the stock they own. They sell these calls to assure a certain but limited gain for their investment. Let's return to the example using SCC. The owner of the $39 SCC common stock may want to lock-in a gain on the stock. By writing (selling) calls, he assures a set amount of profit. The SCC writer promises that he will sell 100 of his shares at $40 apiece. For this promise he may receive $100. If the stock price increases to $43, the writer will still have to sell at $40. Thus, he could miss the opportunity for a $4 per share profit, but he has locked-in a sure $2 per share profit. How? He received $100 for the call and sold the stock for $1 more than its original price of $39 a share. Hence, a $2 profit per share was realized. If the price of SCC stock did not go up enough, the call would expire worthless, and the writer would keep his stock and the small but sure $100 profit. Thus, writing/selling call options is a conservative action; buying calls is more of a gamble.

PUTS

A **put** is just the opposite of a call. The owner of a put expects the price of the stock to decrease. (As mentioned above, the call owner expected the price to increase.) A put works like a call in all other aspects. If the underlying stock does not move in the right direction far enough or fast enough, the owner of the put loses the entire investment. Simply stated, a put is a means by which an investor can profit from a stock which decreases in value.

Options (puts and calls) are very complicated. In addition, new "angles" are being devised all the time. This general information was presented to give you a familiarity with the terms puts and calls.

Commodity Futures

The last specialized money tool we will talk about in this chapter is called **commodity futures** or futures for short. Commodity futures are simply contracts for the buying and selling of various products (commodities) such as wheat, corn, bacon (pork bellies), or gold. The contracts specify that a certain amount of product will be delivered to the contract owners on a certain date at a certain price. The contracts were designed to shift the risk of price drops to investors. A farmer may sell a futures contract on his wheat crop to lock-in today's price. Thus, the farmer can plan on a set price for his wheat. The investor hopes the wheat price will increase and he will be able to make a profit. He is betting on the *future* of wheat, and hence the name commodity futures. Such huge amounts of commodities are involved in each contract that a one cent move in the market price causes tremendous profits or losses. The investors who buy futures contracts seldom if ever accept actual delivery of the commodity—they are simply gambling on the price. Buying and selling commodity futures is a fast-moving and complicated process and is not for beginning investors.

Now we have covered the specialized money tools, hybrid tools, which suit specific needs and wants. If you are considering using these tools, be sure to consult with the experts and acquire a much more in-depth knowledge.

CHAPTER 10

Precious Metals, Collectables, and Real Estate

No writing about investing would be complete without mentioning precious metals, collectables, and real estate. Complete books have been written about each, and you are sure to come across theories proclaiming each of these areas as *the* way to riches. However, each area has drawbacks so serious that direct ownership should not be considered by the average investor. Let's look at these areas one by one.

Directly owning precious metals and gems, such as gold, silver, or diamonds, presents many problems. You must provide for their safekeeping, and there must be a certification of quality and/or grade before purchase *and* sale. When buying, you will pay a premium price above the current market price, and when selling, you will receive a discounted price below market price. If precious metals or gems are attractive to you, consider investments which use the tools already described in previous chapters. Indirect investment in these areas is far less risky than direct ownership. You might purchase the stock of a mining company or of a mutual fund which specializes in one of these areas. Any investment in this area should be no more than a small percentage of your total investment.

Collectables, such as stamps, coins, antiques, and paintings can be fun, but consider them only as a hobby. Investing large sums in collectables should be left to those who are thoroughly knowledgeable and highly experienced. Counterfeit objects and fraudulent practices are not easily recognizable. However, if enough study and time is devoted, collecting can be profitable.

Home ownership is not an investment, it is a necessity—with some very nice side benefits. Buying real estate, other than your personal residence, is not investing; it is starting a business. Selecting, buying, selling, and managing real estate investments is a career, or at least a full-time hobby. To be successful, direct real estate investing requires a lot of time and an in-depth knowledge. True investing can be done on a catch-as-catch-can basis with no need for midnight plumbing fix-ups, vandalism clean-ups, or evictions. A much better way to profit from real estate is through limited partnerships—leave the problems to the professionals and take the profits and tax breaks for yourself.

Direct investing in precious metals and gems, collectables, or real estate should be left to the experts. If you are considering any of these areas for your investment money, use the tools of stocks, mutual funds, or limited partnerships and allow the professionals to earn the profits you can then enjoy.

PART THREE

Your Wealth Building Guide

CHAPTER 11

Planning Your Wealth Building

We are now in the home stretch. You are now familiar with most of the common money terms and tools. We have covered the general factors which will affect your wealth building; we learned that during wealth building you will encounter forces similar to weather elements. Your program must withstand the winds of inflation, the sun-like properties of interest rate changes, and the rain of taxes.

A plan is an extremely important part of your wealth building. It is the blueprint on which all future action is based. This blueprint can show you where to start and guide you step by step. Your wealth building plan must have meaningful detail. It is not enough to simply state "I want to make lots of money," or "I want to be rich." You must spell out the measures to be taken to get you from here to there.

Too many people are planless. The closest many will come to planning for future wants and needs is "to put something away for a rainy day." This vague plan is then carried out using a one-track route to a local passbook account. Life insurance may become a part of this shallow plan by succumbing to the agent's plea to "take care of the wife and kids" or "take this policy—it will provide for your golden years of retirement." Very few consider the growth potential of common stock, and the nearest some come to knowing about bond tools is a pitch from the personnel office to join payroll deduction plans to buy savings bonds. You have an advantage over these people. You already know the hazards, the money terms, and the tools. You have taken the initiative to control your future. Now, let's work together to build a plan.

The Starting Point

A logical place to start your plan is, of course, at the beginning. You will begin your wealth building from where you are right now. But, where are you? How can you figure out a route to where you want to be, if you do not know where you are?

To find your starting point, figure your net worth. What is net worth? It is simply a measurement of your wealth—in this case, your starting wealth. The name, *net worth*, comes from the fact that this is a measure of your worth minus (or net) any liabilities (what you owe). You can find it by adding the value of everything you own and then subtracting what you owe. This value will show you how much money you would hold in your hand after you sold everything and paid all amounts owed. For example, if you owned a home, car, had $5,000 in savings, and $500 in a checking account, the calculation might look like this:

House (market value)	$60,000.00	
Car (market value)	4,000.00	
Savings	5,000.00	
Checking	500.00	
(Worth)		$69,500.00

Mortgage	$40,000.00	
Car Loan (balance)	2,000.00	
Credit Card (balance)	100.00	
(Liabilities)		−$42,100.00
NET WORTH		$27,400.00

Be sure your net worth calculations give you a realistic picture. Fudging the figures fools only yourself. How much is that furniture really worth? Are some pieces of furniture antiques? What about the stereo? Do not forget to include everything. Make this snapshot of where you stand as clear as possible; give it some time and thought. Go through this exercise at least once a year to enable you to see "how you are doing" with your wealth building. Most people are very pleasantly surprised at the "bottom line" of their net worth.

The Footing

Now you know your starting point. The next step is to provide something you need during all phases of your wealth building program—protection. You must protect yourself and family from all the forms of adversity that may come your way. Including protection in your plan is like making sure of the footing for your building. Don't build your hopes for the future on the shifting sands of fate. Provide the protection and sound footing that the various forms of insurance can supply.

Insurance should be thought of as a means of shifting the risk of unacceptable losses to someone else. Your plan will not withstand the losses caused by uncontrollable events; therefore, it is essential that you insure against these harmful happenings and shift the risk to insurance companies. Probably, the first type of insurance that comes to mind is life insurance. Obviously, the death of the breadwinner means the end of income. Without life insurance this lack of income can add economic disaster to personal tragedy.

You should consider only "pure" protection—term insurance; there are far better methods of accumulating cash than in a life insurance policy. Another happening that can stop income is disability, so disability insurance is a must. Also, realize that medical costs have increased drastically. There is no need to insure for the little bumps and bruises, but major medical protection from the breaks and operations is another must. Do not overlook the fact that without liability insurance, when simply driving your car down the street you may run into a law suit that could spell disaster for your wealth building plans. So, liability insurance, too, is a must.

Some of the protection mentioned above may be provided by your employer. Many states require worker's compensation, a form of disability insurance. If the insurance provided in the areas we just discussed is not adequate or is non-existant, get your own. Your entire wealth building program depends on adequate protection.

The Foundation

You are now assured of a good footing for your building. Now you can actually plan the structure itself. The first part, the foundation, is obviously critical. The foundation prevents the entire structure from collapsing in the earth shaking event that you become unemployed. Is your job secure? Do not be too sure; many of the unemployed also thought their jobs were secure. Some protection against unemployment may be realized in the form of unemployment insurance from your state. However, it is seldom enough. Full protection must be provided by maintaining an emergency fund.

An emergency fund is simply a sum of money set aside but readily accessible, to be used to pay expenses during unemployment. It can also provide for other unexpected emergencies such as no-notice cross-country trips to aid sick relatives. The amount in this fund should cover no less than six (6) months' expenses. To find the specific sum you need, add up your current *essential* expenses. Some expenses will be eliminated if you lose your job; others will not. Include only those which are essential. Update these figures at least once a year. To store the money for this fund, make use of money market tools offered by most banks and many mutual funds. (To refresh your memory about these tools simply refer back to the appropriate section(s) of this book.) Once the emergency fund is established, you have assured a solid foundation for your wealth building. Now we can proceed to the part of your blueprint that is the most interesting and fun: the actual form, shape, and substance of your proposed wealth structure—your goals.

The Structure

We are now at a point where, by setting definite goals, you can give your wealth structure a form. These goals will actually be the substance of the wealth building. During this goal setting process, you must free your mind from the limitations of the "impossible now." You must consider everything that you want or need and put aside the thought that it may be "impossible now." Make a list of *all* the things you want or need—the *things* you want or need. These are the things money can buy. To have money itself as a goal is not enough. You may, however, wish to have the sense of security that a large reserve fund offers, but this must be only one of several goals. List them all. What do you *really* want? The list should be limited only by your capacity to dream. The list you make may look something like this:

A home of our own	College for kids
A second car (third?)	Security of a
Travel	reserve fund
Comfortable retirement	New furniture
Tennis club membership	

Hopefully, your list will be longer, but this gives you the idea. Also, your list must be much more detailed. For example, a home should be spelled out in as much detail as possible, i.e., a new $150,000, 3 bedroom, 2 bath, ranch style with a view. Detailed descriptions of your goals will help you visualize the things you are working for. They will give you the encouragement to go on with the program. Each day you will be getting closer to your specific goals—you will be able to say, "This I do for my beautiful house with a view!"

Once your goal list is complete, rank each item in order of importance *to you*. By doing this, you can work for the most important goals first. Is the new furniture more important than a new car? The decision is yours. It may help you to make your decision if you consider the side benefits provided by some of your goals. For example, buying your own home is very profitable as well as pleasurable. The interest and taxes paid on the property are sweet income tax deductions. If you choose wisely, the rising market value of your house will steadily increase your net worth. With comfortable retirement as a goal, you will not have to worry about the availability or adequacy of Social Security. In any case, planning for your retirement is very important. If *you* do not provide for retirement, who will? You may very well enjoy being elderly and well-off, but being old and poor is sad and preventable. Plan for your retirement now.

Your blueprint is now complete. Your wealth building is made up of all the wants, dreams, needs, and pleasures represented by your goals. (Some goals will change as you progress through life. Review them periodically to keep your blueprint up-to-date.)

The Material

What and where is the material you will use for the construction of your wealth building? The material you will use is money. It should be provided from present reserves and/or a savings program. This program must have three characteristics: It must be predictable, regular, and as automatic as possible. To be predictable, the sums saved must come out of the spending stream before all other living expenses. If you rely on an amount "left over at the end of the month," you are flirting with failure. The first person paid should be *you* and then take care of the others. Make this predictable amount a percentage of your monthly income—as much as is possible, but at least 5%. Be sure you have left enough to live on, but remember, the more you can contribute,the faster your project will proceed. When determining the amount to set aside it is good to remember that every $100 saved will bring you $100 closer to your new car, new home, etc. Recall the goals each time you set aside another sum. Also, you should use any method you can to make the deposit automatic. If it can occur without thought, so much the better. Again, the requirement is for a predictable (5% minimum) regular (at least monthly) amount taken out of the spending stream as automatically as possible.

These monies can be put to work in the same type of money market tools that you should be using for your emergency fund. Banks and mutual funds provide you with some of the choices. Once the steady flow of material for your wealth building project has begun, the planning stage is over. You now have a beautiful blueprint, and the money is on the way. The building can now begin!

As you start to build, you must decide what tools to use for each different job. Choosing, in many cases, will simply be a matter of remembering what the particular money tool was designed to do. However, some choices will depend on your judgment of risk.

Risk

Risk is the only difference between some tools. You may buy call options and double your money in only a short time, or you may buy T-bills which give only a small but sure profit. The difference between these two short-term money tools is like day and night because of the difference in risk. Let's look more closely at this element, for many of your decisions will depend on your understanding and acceptance of risk.

Risk is defined as the possiblity of loss. In Chapter 1, we talked about some of the hazards you encounter in the world of money. The forces of inflation and interest rate changes are both risks. You must consider them when you decide on a course of action. Even if you decide to do nothing, you will encounter risk. If you do not save, you risk your freedom, i.e., you may become dependent on the government for your support. If you save, but only stuff your money under the mattress, you risk the loss of all to theft, or fire, or inflation. Risk is ever-present and inevitable.

The amount of risk that is acceptable is different for each person. As you proceed with your wealth building, the amount of risk you can accept will change. If the amount of money saved is small and your needs are large, you must be more careful than when the reverse is true. You can take more chances when you are young, rich, or not depended upon than if you are older, poorer, or financially responsible for others. The person with seven children can not accept as much risk as a person with a working spouse and no children. Money needed soon should not be exposed to as much risk as money with no immediate need. For instance, if you just barely have your child's education cost saved and it is payable in six months, you would not use it to purchase stock; for the market may have a temporary downturn leaving you no time to recover. However, if the tuition is in hand and the child is only six years old, you would be wise to buy a good quality stock. Your tuition money may double or triple by college time. So you see, each individual and circumstance can accept different risk.

Whenever possible, diversify! This means simply not to keep all your eggs in one basket. Diversifying minimizes risk. Use the banks, and stocks, and mutual funds. When buying stock, buy shares of different companies in different lines of work. This diversification assures you that even if one stock turns sour or one tool proves to be a bad choice, all will not be lost. It may limit the speed of your growth, but it will also limit your losses.

Flexibility

You must be flexible as your project progresses; you must be ready to change the tool or tools in use. Are the winds of inflation roaring again? Have interest rates decreased to unprofitable levels? Does the rain of taxes threaten to wash out profits? Is your family situation changing? Are you in the stage of an early family, or the time after the children have grown and left, or retirement? All these situations may require different tools. As you go through life you must be flexible in your selection of these tools and must switch between them as the situation changes. Do not become "married" to a bank account or a particular stock—stay with a tool only as long as it is profitable and appropriate to your situation.

CHAPTER 12

How to Use Money Tools

The next thing you will realize is that you will need the help of some experts. Using the advice and knowledge of a banker, broker, or taxperson is much the same as using plumbers, electricians, and carpenters in a building program. Some tasks you may be able to handle yourself while others are done best by the experts. Establish a team of experts you can call on to handle those tasks that you do not have the time, talent, or energy to do. The following information will help you choose your team.

Choosing Your Team

All the members of your team should have certain general characteristics. First, every member should be compatible with you. You both must "talk the same language"—your expert should be easy to talk to and understand. If he too often talks in specialized terms that are over your head, find another expert. Secondly, your team must be generous with information so you can learn and make better money making decisions. Third, there must be a feeling that each is a member of your team, with your interest at heart. Thinking and talking in terms of "we" and "us" is what you should watch for here, i.e., "We would benefit from this" or, "That action would be good for us." It is also important that the relationship with your team members be fun. There is a place for a sense of humor in business. Business can be awfully dull without it—why not enjoy it as you go along?

A good place to start looking for experts is by asking friends. They may already know someone who can help you. You possibly may have an expert as a friend; however, this closeness may present some problems. If all else fails, you can turn to the yellow pages. Here, your selection will be based on convenience and, hopefully, reputation. If the firm is close and has a good reputation, give it a try. Remember at all times, *you* are hiring the team. If you are not satisfied, fire them.

What you need in the form of tax accountants and insurance agents is obvious, and if you follow the general guidelines above, there should be no problem in finding and selecting suitable ones. Bank managers, on the other hand, will tend to come and go through transfers and promotions, so you may have to go through the selection process more than once. Choose one that will take the time to talk with you and return your phone calls.

Broker/Brokerage House Selection

A stockbroker expert may have the title of Registered Representative, Account Executive, or Broker. As mentioned in the section on stocks, a broker is the person who arranges the buying and selling of stocks, bonds, and mutual funds. He works for a company known in general terms as a brokerage house (Merrill Lynch, E. F. Hutton, etc.). A broker can buy and sell as you direct him. He has access to all the "machinery" that makes this possible.

When selecting a broker, it is a good idea to choose an experienced one with a good track record, i.e., someone who has "been around" and lived through the ups and downs of the market. This type will not be overly optimistic in a bull (up) market and will not panic in a bear (down) market. He is more likely to survive in his job, and, therefore, will serve you better over the long run. The brokerage firm he works for should have a strong reputation and also have strong possibilities of surviving. It can be quite traumatic to deal with a firm that ends up going out of business.

As mentioned before, the selection may start with referrals from trusted friends, or fellow workers, or from the yellow pages. Narrow the choices down to two or three and visit them. If you can not visit them, phone them and talk for a while. Your first objective is to see if you both talk on the same "wave-length" and are compatible. Ask if the brokerage firm is a member of SIPC, which we will discuss later, and ask about the services the firm can provide. Find out what the broker thinks about current happenings in the world of money such as inflation, interest rates, or general stock market moves.

If the brokerage firm provides a research service, ask for copies of its research reports. Firms which provide this research service, study the companies which offer stocks and bonds, and they judge their investment suitability. The written research reports will outline the findings and will usually contain buy/sell recommendations. Ask for the last five copies of research reports that the brokerage firm has produced. Requesting the last five will assure that the broker can not select only the best. These reports will give you a fair idea about the quality and depth of the research service.

While you are sizing him up, the broker should also be trying to find out about you. You will be questioned about your goals and your feelings about risk. The questioning, your research, and your impressions should enable you to make a good decision about which broker and brokerage firm you should use.

FULL-SERVICE OR DISCOUNT

Another choice you will have is between a firm offering full brokerage services and one which simply processes your orders to buy or sell. The full-service organizations provide research, advice, and assistance; the discount houses do not. The commission charged by a broker in a full-service brokerage is fixed and is higher than the commission you will pay at discount brokerage houses. The generic name of "discount house" comes from the fact that these brokerages "discount" or reduce the commission or fee that they charge. To illustrate the difference in commissions let's compare a purchase of 100 shares of stock valued at $30 a share. (Realize that this is only an example—your actual charge will vary with the type of tool used and the amount of purchase.) On 100 shares at $30 a share, the full-service broker may charge approximately

$70, or 2.3%. The discount broker's charge can be as low as $30, or 1%.

Discount houses have access to the same market "machinery" as the full-service houses. In other words, their ability to buy and sell is the same as that of a full-service broker. The discount broker does not, however, offer research, advice, recommendations, or opinions to investors who may need these additional services. If you know the company you want to invest in, the number of shares you want to buy, and exactly what you want to do, the discount broker can do it for you. Some full-service houses will negotiate commissions for large investors with "self directed accounts."

ACCOUNT TYPES

The broker you select can advise you on the details of setting up an account. There are many types available with different legal and/or tax considerations. There are two general account types with which you should be familiar—a cash account and a margin account. In a cash account, you simply pay for everything in full. With a margin account, you can buy "on margin." When you buy "on margin," you pay only part of the cost, and the brokerage firm provides the extra (margin) money needed for the purchase. In other words, they will loan you part of the cost of purchase, and they will charge you interest on the loan.

When you buy on margin you must be prepared to provide additional money to satisfy a maintenance call. A maintenance call is issued to investors whose stock was bought on margin and has since decreased in value. In essence, the stock acts as collateral for the loan. The brokerage house will ask you to maintain the value of this collateral and will issue a maintenance call if the stock value falls below a certain amount. You would then have to add more money to the account or sell the stock and take the loss. Most brokerage houses require that a margin account contain a minimum amount. Therefore, this type of account is not available to smaller investors. The beginner should stick to cash accounts, anyway. After you gain some experience and confidence, you can always switch from cash to margin.

WORKING WITH YOUR BROKER

Your broker can not tell you what to buy or sell; however, a full-service broker can provide you with a lot of valuable information and advise you on buying and selling. Your full-service broker can and should provide you with the facts on which he bases his recommendations. These facts will pertain to the company's earnings, market price, history, and recent developments.

Your broker can also help you decide when to buy or sell. Timing your purchase or sale to coincide with the ups and downs of the market is a difficult task, but the effort can make a big difference in profits. The addage "buy low, sell high" still holds true. Do not be overly disappointed if you do not actually catch the peaks or valleys; you still will do well if the purchase was made close to the low or the sale close to the high. Once again, your broker can advise and assist you; however, the final decision is yours.

After you make the decision as to what and when to buy, you must decide how many. This will depend heavily on the price and your available money, but remember diversification (eggs not all in one basket). Your final order will either be for a round lot or an odd lot. A round lot is any multiple of 100 shares (200, 500, etc.). An odd lot is less than 100 shares. An order for 150 shares is a round lot and an odd lot. There sometimes is an additional charge for odd lot orders. If you intend to do odd lot business, check to find out if there is an additional cost.

HOLDING YOUR CERTIFICATES

There are three ways to deal with the certificates which you decide to buy or sell. You may personally hold them, assign custody to someone else, or allow the brokerage house to handle them. The best method for you depends on your psychological makeup and generally how you like to operate. If you accept the certificates yourself, you avoid any risk of an accounting error by your broker. You would also have ready access to the certificates if you need to use them as loan collateral. You must, however, provide for their safekeeping, and this usually means inconvenient trips to the bank safe deposit box. When you sell, you would then have to return to the bank, get the certificates, and deliver them to the broker for transfer to the new owner. Some prefer this sure control and do not mind the inconvenience.

Those who receive the certificates from their broker sometimes assign custody of them to others. This may be done, for example, if you hold your own certificates but need to travel. You could then sell the certificates while you are away by signing and sending a stock power to the custodian. A *stock power* is a legal form authorizing the sale of the specific stock. This form, when attached to the certificate, enables the sale the same as if you signed the actual certificate. Your banker, attorney, or broker can act as custodian for your certificates. It is more convenient to assign custody to your broker, for this does away with the need to deliver the certificates.

Most certificates are handled by brokers in *street name accounts.* These accounts eliminate the need for you to accept and safeguard the certificates and then deliver them again when you want to sell. The certificates will be kept by your broker and remain in your brokerage firm's name. The broker will give you a statement of your account periodically, and this statement is proof that you are the owner of record.

PROTECTION FOR YOUR BROKERAGE ACCOUNT

The U.S. Congress, in 1970, created the Securities Investor Protection Corporation (SIPC). This corporation operates in much the same fashion as the FDIC and FSLIC insurance for banks. Under SIPC, brokerage accounts are insured for up to $100,000, of which $40,000 can be cash. This protection does not cover stock price declines. The aim of this insurance is to protect you in the event of bankruptcy of your brokerage firm. It has been thoroughly tested; the SIPC has handled thousands of liquidations since its inception. Most of these were small, regional firms. Investors received payments promptly in all cases except margin accounts which had some losses because of complications arising from their loans. All other accounts were cleared without a hitch. SIPC coverage is a must for street name accounts. Not all brokerage houses subscribe to this coverage; check with yours. In addition to SIPC coverage, some brokerage houses provide ·surance which will protect investors with as much as $500,000 on account. If your invested sums approach this size, consider using a brokerage which provides that protection.

The Need for a Financial Planner

As you proceed with your wealth building program, you may or may not need the services of a *Financial Planner*. A decade ago this profession did not formally exist; now there are an estimated 7,500 personal financial planners. If your net worth is $100,000 or more and your income is $35,000, a financial planner can be of great assistance in your wealth building. Here is a professional who can fit together the pieces of your personal wealth building puzzle. He has a background in many areas including insurance, tax shelters, trusts, and stocks and bonds. If necessary, he has access to many specialists in these areas. A planner can provide you with a complete wealth building blueprint. He/she can also help assure the flow of money into your building project by providing a budget for your spending and investment sums.

The fee charged by the planner will be based on the complexity of your personal situation and the amount of your income and assets. The fee may be $1,000 to $8,000 for a master plan, or if the planner is allowed to accept commissions on the sale of some of the money tools suggested in the plan, it could be less. A yearly follow-up will cost $200 or more. A financial planner can be used for just specific problems for an hourly fee of $50 to $150. These fees for tax and investment advice are *tax deductible.*

Financial planning services are also provided by some bank trust departments and insurance and mutual fund companies. Be cautious about using these services. Banks have been providing planning service for some of the wealthy for generations; however, bank trust departments tend to be extremely conventional and conservative. These were good tactics at one time, but they fail to keep pace with rapidly changing inflation, interest rates, and taxes. Some insurance companies and mutual fund companies will mass produce computer-generated plans to attract new customers. In most cases, you will find these plans shallow and of little help.

FINDING A FINANCIAL PLANNER

If you have exhausted the leads from friends and acquaintances, here are two associations which may help you find a planner (the associations' addresses follow this writing). The first one, the ICFP, will send you the names of all the planners in your area who have earned the designation of Certified Financial Planner (CFP). To earn this designation, the planner must pass courses covering insurance, taxes, employee benefit and pension programs, investments, and estate planning. Also listed will be the planner's education, experience, and fees. The second association, the IAFP, will send you the names of three of their associates who operate in your area.

When you are checking the names of your possible planners, look for those with high education, credentials such as brokers' or real estate licenses, and/or registration as an investment advisor with the Securities and Exchange Commission. The one you choose should have access to any needed expert information and a computer.

FINANCIAL PLANNING ASSOCIATIONS

The Institute of Certified Financial
   Planners (ICFP)
9725 E. Hampden Ave.
Denver, CO 80231

The International Association for
   Financial Planning (IAFP)
5775 Peachtree Dunwood Rd.
Suite 120C
Atlanta, GA 30342

The Need for an Attorney

You should select an attorney using the guidelines we discussed when we talked about selecting your other team members. The ease of communications is probably more important with your attorney than with others. Legal terminology is stiff, staid, and very difficult to understand. If you find an attorney who will translate it and use understandable language, you've got a winner. The reason legal terms are so hard to understand is that each word and phrase has survived the tests of the courts, and new, updated, or simpler terms would require needless further testing. Thus, we will forever be "parties of the first part." An attorney can at least make sure that you understand the language.

You will need an attorney to set up any trusts that will be a part of your wealth program. There are two basic types of trusts that are important. Let's look at the two types, one at a time.

TESTAMENTARY TRUST

The familiar term for this type of trust is a will. Your last will and testament is a very important part of your wealth program. Without a will, you surrender your right to decide how your wealth will be distributed. Without a will, the state decides. Your property and the well-being of your family are at stake. A will (a testamentary trust) is essential. Some people draw up their own wills, and sometimes these wills perform as written. Do not take chances with this important document —use an attorney.

When the provisions of a will are to be carried out, they are first reviewed by a probate court. The court makes sure everything is proper and legal and that all instructions are followed. Probate is time-consuming and expensive; however, your wishes will be fulfilled.

LIVING TRUST

You may wish to have a living trust in place of, or in addition to, a will. A living trust is in effect while you live and simply continues in effect after death. It is very similar to a will in many ways. The biggest advantage of this trust is that it avoids probate and thus minimizes the cost and time lags in the settlement of your estate. It can be written under the law of the state in which you live, or the state where the property is located, or the state where the beneficiary lives.

There are many different kinds of living trusts designed to accomplish different purposes. Most are designed to operate as tax shelters or to handle educational funds, charitable contributions, family support, and the like. Your attorney can supply you with the details about the different types of living trusts. Check them out.

Now you have some guidelines to help you select and work with your team. Use these team members for the highly technical tasks in which they specialize. Your wealth building program will be better for it. Let's turn next to the arena you and your team will inevitably be working in during your wealth building program—the Stock Market.

The Stock Market

The Stock Market is the collective term which includes all the organizations engaged in the buying and selling of stock, bonds, and mutual fund shares. The Stock Market is gigantic; it includes the investments of over 25 million people as well as investments of institutions like insurance companies, banks, and pension funds. The best known part of the Stock Market is the New York Stock Exchange; there are over 27,000,000,000 (billion) shares of stock listed on the New York Exchange alone. The exchanges are an all-important part of the American economy. Let's now look at the largest ones.

THE EXCHANGES

There are two major exchanges and other smaller regional ones. The New York Stock Exchange (NYSE) and the American Stock Exchange (AMEX) are the two largest. Exchanges provide a central clearing house for the nation-wide buying and selling of stocks and bonds. Exchanges deal only with those companies which meet certain financial standards. For example, the New York exchange requires that a company issue a minimum of one million shares. Issues (stocks and bonds) that qualify for trading on exchanges are called "listed." This stems from the fact that exchanges report prices and volume of trades to the media by "listing" the issues. The goal of many companies is to be "listed" on a major exchange, and yet, other companies qualify for listing and do not want it. (Your investment decision should not be based on whether or not an issue is listed.) Those companies who do not qualify and those who decide against listing are traded over-the-counter (OTC). The OTC market is essentially a telephone/ computer network. Buy and sell action is negotiated over the network instead of on the trading floor of an exchange. Realize that a broker can make purchases for you in the OTC as well as the NYSE, AMEX, and other exchanges.

STOCK MARKET BAROMETERS

There are five companies that show what is happening in the Stock Market. Each company reports on a different group of stocks. The reports show the general trend of stock prices in the different groups. The most often quoted is the Dow Jones Industrial Average. The media is referring to this average when they say, "The Stock Market climbed 10 points today in active trading." The reports of all five companies are covered below.

(1) **The Dow Jones Averages:**

Dow Jones Industrial Average—Average of the market values of 30 separate stocks. These combined stocks account for 20% of the value of all common stock on the NYSE.

Dow Jones Utilities Average–Average market value of 15 gas and electric companies.

Dow Jones Transportation Average–Average market value of 20 firms in the railroad, airline, and trucking industries.

Dow Jones Average of 65 Stocks–A combination of the first three.

(2) **Standard and Poor's 500 Stocks:**

An index (mathmatical computation) which tracks the value of the shares of 500 companies.

(3) **New York Stock Exchange Index:**

A computation of the value of all common stock listed on the NYSE.

(4) **American Stock Exchange Index:**

Same as above except it's for the American Exchange (AMEX).

(5) **NASDAQ Index** (pronounced nas' dak):

National Association of Security Dealers Automated Quotations. A computation of 2,350 common shares in the OTC market.

The averages just discussed will indicate general movements in prices, but specific issues may or may not conform to this general movement. Some issues will go up or down in value for no other reason than the fact that the general market went up or down. Other issues will move in the opposite direction of the averages. As a rule, however, when the stock market averages change, most individual stocks will change in the same direction.

Information Needs

The more information you have, the better your selection and buy/sell decisions will be. You need general business information and detailed facts about specific companies. General information is the starting point. It will show you what is happening in various parts of the business world and with the economy in general. You should look for things like building and construction trends, how well autos are selling, and rising home computer sales. You should also watch for reports on changes in inflation, interest rates, and tax laws. This general type of information should lead you to the more promising industries and help you avoid those that are in for hard times.

Once you have an idea of the general direction you should move, you will then need specific information on companies. Do not forget your broker is a valuable source of this information. The sort of details you need are about recent price movements, earnings history, and reports of profits. Watch for significant company happenings like management changes, new product introductions, expansion plans, and lawsuit troubles. Good wealth building decisions depend on good general and specific information.

INFORMATION SOURCES

Business information comes in many shapes, sizes, and prices. Let's consider the available sources starting with the least expensive. Among the least expensive are reports in your local daily newspaper or on radio and TV broadcasts. These sources can provide much valuable information. The local daily newspaper usually has a section devoted to business happenings. Most will report recent prices of stock issues traded that day and will comment on the averages. Radio stations frequently offer special business segments on regular newscasts, and "all-news" radio usually offers in-depth business reports. If you receive public supported TV broadcasts, watch the "Nightly Business Report" carried daily and the weekly "Wall Street Week."

Specialized business publications are more expensive but will give you broader coverage and a more in-depth look. Two excellent newspaper publications are *The Wall Street Journal* and *Barrons.* You can read the *Barrons* on the week-end when it comes out and during the week catch one or two copies of the *Journal.* Two outstanding business related magazines are *Business Week* and the monthly publication of *Money* magazine.

INVESTMENT ADVISORY SUBSCRIPTION SERVICES

The most highly specialized and costly source of information comes from Investment Advisory Services. Your subscription to these services will bring you periodic newsletter type publications. These newsletters will have one to five pages of information such as news, companies' estimated earnings, statistics, analyses, advice about investment strategies, and recommended lists of stocks. A typical subscription costs $65 to $175 and is *tax deductible.* If your wealth building program has progressed to at least the $15,000 investment point, a good service can be helpful. Those with over $100,000 to invest would benefit from taking several services. You will find that these services will follow one of two basic approaches to investment analysis. One is called the *technical approach* the other is the *fundamental approach.* Those who follow the technical approach to market analysis study past performance. They are sometimes called *chartists* because they keep charts and graphs of market activity and base decisions on the patterns formed on the charts. Their basic theory is, "If it happened before, it will happen again." The fundamental approach studies the basic financial health of a company or industry and bases decisions on forecasts of sales, profits or earnings, and the like. Neither approach is

100% right or wrong, and the best approach to use is probably some combination of the two. Advisory services may be one extreme or the other or may use a combination approach.

To find the service you are most comfortable with, send for a free catalogue from the "Select Information Exchange," 2095 Broadway, New York, NY 10023. This catalogue describes hundreds of services and offers trial subscriptions to a certain number for a very small fee. For example, you may be offered 20 trials for $15. This is a good way to sample the services and find out which one suits you.

Listed below are some of the better known services. The first three have the largest circulation. The last three are exceptional values. Remember, the costs are all *tax deductible.* Also, you may find some of these publications at your broker's.

(1) *The Value Line*
    Investment Survey
    711 Third Avenue
    New York, NY 10017
    (weekly—$330/yr)

(2) *The Outlook*
    Standard & Poor's Corp.
    25 Broadway
    New York, NY 10004
    (weekly—$145/yr)

(3) *United Business &*
    Investment Report
    United Business Service
    210 Newberry St.
    Boston, MA 02116
    (weekly—$150/yr)

(4) *Smart Money*
    The Hirsch
    Organization, Inc.
    6 Deer Trail
    Old Tappen, NJ 07675
    (monthly + bulletins
    —$85/yr)

(5) *Market logic*
    Institute for Econometric
    Research, Inc.
    3471 N. Federal Hwy.
    Fort Lauderdale, FL 33306
    (bi-weekly—$68/yr)

(6) *The Johnson Survey*
    John S. Herold, Inc.
    35 Mason St.
    Greenwich, CT 06830
    (monthly—$78/yr)

CHAPTER 13

Making Your Moves

You now have a good feel for the language and tools of the world of money. You have a well-thought-out blueprint to guide your wealth building efforts and a steady flow of money to supply "material." You know about the risks involved and the required flexibility. You know your team of experts will help you with special building problems. You are familiar with the market, your information needs, and sources.

You are now ready to make your move—but which direction should you go? The forces of taxes and inflation will help direct you. If the winds of inflation are picking up speed, you should invest in "things" which increase in value with inflation—stocks and real estate, possibly in the form of limited partnerships, work well. Money will decrease in value, and investments in debt issues (bonds, CDs, etc.) will not do well. In periods of high inflation you should *own* not *loan.* You should meet tax increases, caused by either changes in the law or your personal situation, with moves to tax shelters, tools with tax deferrals, or trusts.

Your next step depends on how comfortable you are making investment decisions. You may decide to direct your own investments and rely on your own knowledge and evaluation of information, or you may decide to strictly follow the advice and recommendations of your broker, financial planner, or other such expert. Remember, however, the experts can only advise and recommend. The final decision and consequences are yours. It is best to use a combination of the first two methods. You should develop your own general leads and then turn to the experts for specific guidance.

Happenings Can Help

When looking for your general leads, you will find it helpful to watch the happenings in the world around you. You should notice both the positive and the negative happenings. The positive happenings will direct you to profitable investments, while the negative ones will help you avoid wrong investment decisions. The rapid growth of the cable TV industry would be an example of a positive happening. It leads you to an area where profits may be enjoyed. An example of a negative would be the happenings with nuclear power generators. If you see that construction of new generators is plagued with cost over-runs and that there are serious problems with state and federal regulators and environmental groups, investments in utilities with nuclear projects may be inappropriate at that time. The world around you will provide you with general leads if you just remain alert to its signals.

After you have found your general leads by paying attention to the forces and watching the happenings, you can then turn to the experts for specific guidance. For example, your information may tell you that a particular industry has a rosy future. You could then take this lead to a broker to decide on a specific company in that industry. For instance, you learn that home computers are selling so well that there are estimates that every home will have one within the next decade. You go to your broker and ask for information on companies that will profit from the computer boom. The broker provides you with research reports and his opinion on three leading companies. You read this information, consider the opinion, and select the one company that "sounds" the best to you. Following the path from general leads, to specific choices, to investment decisions will guide you to success.

Keys to Successful Investments

Good investment decisions also depend on your familiarity with several key do's and dont's. These rules, resulting from trial and error, have withstood the test of time and will be as valid tomorrow as they are today and have been for generations.

TRENDS NOT FADS

You should be looking for trends as you observe what is happening around you. At the same time, you must avoid fads. The difference between these two terms is durability. A trend can produce profits over a long run; however, a fad is short-lived. A fad is extremely risky because split-second and complicated investment decisions may be required. Trends develop slowly and enable studied and thorough evaluations. Some examples will clarify these terms. The recent CB radio fad produced wild and exaggerated enthusiasm. Hundreds of new companies, manufacturing and/or selling CB radios, appeared almost over-night. Unwary investors, who wanted to hop on the bandwagon, were faced with the complicated choice between all these new and yet unproven companies. When the CB fad began to fade, many investors also saw their investments fade. Only those who were lucky enough to choose the right company and bought soon enough and sold before it was too late were able to profit. Do not allow your success to depend on such chancy decisions—avoid fads.

Trends offer leads with much better possibilities than fads. For instance, you may have noticed the growing use of robots in manufacturing. Robotronics may hold the promise of use on most production lines. This type of lead could give you the time to select one of the few companies who stand to profit from the trend. Development of this trend will not be an over-night process. The new robots must be researched, designed, and developed. The companies that already have them in use are profiting from their sales now and will continue to profit as they constantly improve their product. These companies can provide investors with profits over the long run, and timing of the buy/sell decision is not critical. Look for trends; they will lead to successful wealth building.

LONG RUN NOT FOREVER

Do invest for the long run, but don't fall in love with your investment. Patience with your investments is a must; marriage to them is a mistake. Too often, investors get the jitters about momentary fluctuations in the value of their investments. Price changes occur daily or even hourly, and buy/sell decisions based on such short-term price swings are unsound. Your investment decision should be based on the good future prospects of a company that is selected for its financial soundness. In and out trading, day to day, works for some experienced professionals, but most successful investors must plan on the long run. Many large gains have been lost when investors were too quick to take small profits or when they sold during a temporary downturn.

Investing for the long run does not mean accepting investments for better or worse. Stick with them only as long as the reasons you originally selected them remain valid, and only as long as they are performing as expected. Review investments periodically and weed-out poor performers. These reviews should not be daily and need not be weekly, but ever so often check to see if there have been any significant changes.

DIVERSIFY BUT NOT BLINDLY

No matter how many other tactics you try, remember you must diversify. Spreading your investments spreads your risk and eliminates the possibility of a total wipe-out. Diversify by investing in a variety of companies in different industries and by using different money tools. If one element in your portfolio (collection of investments) turns bad, others should hold up. Another good way to diversify is to use the mutual fund money tool, but even here it is best to diversify and use different funds. Diversification is a must, but watch what you are doing. Do not invest in something that is going nowhere just for the sake of diversity. Also, you must pay attention to what is happening with the forces of inflation, interest rates, and taxes. For example, if interest rates are bound to rise, investing in bonds simply for diversification is foolish. If the steel industry is reeling under foreign competition, investing in it may not be a wise choice. Spread your investment among sound companies with good prospects and use a variety of tools appropriate to the times. The table below will serve well as a memory jogger for these important DOs and DON'Ts of good investing.

KEYS TO SUCCESSFUL INVESTMENTS	
DO	**DON'T**
WATCH FOR TRENDS	FOLLOW FADS
INVEST FOR LONG RUN	FALL IN LOVE WITH INVESTMENTS
DIVERSIFY	IGNORE HAPPENINGS OR FORCES*

*Happenings in the world around you or the forces of inflation, interest rates, and taxes.

The Practice Plunge

A good way to test the investment waters is to take a practice plunge. This is simple, fun, and educational. As you start with your wealth building program, try this at least once before you make the first actual move. Let's try the stock market. Select some issues, perhaps from your local newspaper, and give it your best shot. Use all the tips, tactics, and techniques described in this book. Decide to "buy" shares of companies with a set amount of imaginary money. Write down the purchase prices so you can track your results. Now, simply watch what happens. As the weeks pass, check the prices. How did you do? Would you have made money on your selections? If not, why not? Maybe you had insufficient information or were following a fad instead of a trend. Whatever the reason, you now have the opportunity to "fine tune" your selection process without any actual risk. Even if you "made money" you can now figure ways to increase profits for the next practice or the real thing. Either way, a practice plunge will help to assure your successful wealth building program.

Begin Now

We have come a long way. We have covered the basics of the world of money, step by step. Although this writing now comes to an end, I sincerely hope that this is just the beginning for you. Everyone needs to have a working knowledge of the world of money. You now have this knowledge and a well-thought-out plan. Be alert to opportunities to expand and improve your wealth building knowledge. Many other fine publications exist that are devoted to increasing this knowledge. Beware of get-rich-quick schemes and books that advocate investment approaches which are too narrow and do not recognize the wide variety of money tools available. Use the knowledge you have gained here to guide you through the maze of other publications. It will serve you well.

You are now ready to start your program to acquire all the things "dreamed of and hoped for." I urge you to begin now; tomorrow is always a day away.

PART FOUR

Your
Quick-Reference
Dictionary

Your Quick-Reference Dictionary

This part of your book can serve two purposes. First, it can serve as a review of the information we have covered in other sections of this book, and second, it will serve as a money language dictionary. Presented here are definitions, in alphabetical order, of the terms you will use and hear as you begin to operate in the world of money. If you have forgotten the meaning of a term you come across while wealth building, turn to this section to refresh your memory.

Account Executive

A title for some brokers. (See Stockbroker.)

Advisory Service

An information service offered to investors for a fee. The information frequently includes buy/sell advice.

American Stock Exchange (AMEX)

The second largest U.S. center (exchange) where stocks, bonds, and mutual funds are bought and sold. (See New York Stock Exchange.)

Annual Report

A report, issued yearly to investors, that shows a company's financial status and plans for the future.

Annuity

Insurance companies offer this money tool. It is designed to pay you a safe, sure, and regular amount of income, usually after retirement. You pay the company a set amount, either in a lump sum or a series of payments, and the company will pay interest on what you invest. The interest paid is tax-deferred until you begin receiving payments from the company at retirement. The interest paid may be fixed and unchangeable, as in the case of a *fixed annuity*, or may fluctuate, as in the case of a *variable annuity*. The payments continue for as long as you live.

Ask/Asking Price

The price you will pay. (See Bid Price.)

Assets

Everything a person or a company owns. (See Liabilities, Net Assets.)

Baby Bond

A bond with less than a $1,000 face value.

Banker's Acceptance

A short-term money market tool offered by banks and used chiefly by large organizations. The money, in denominations of at least $100,000, earns a specific amount of interest, is secured by the acceptance, and matures in 270 days or less.

Bear/Bear Market

Bear—Someone who believes the stock market will decline. Bear Market—A declining market. Memory Aid—The bear's claws point down. (See Bull/Bull Market.)

Bearer Bond

A bond that is not recorded in the bondholder's name. Anyone who presents (bears) the bond or the bond coupon for payment will be paid. (See Bond, Coupon, Registered Bond.)

Bid Price

In mutual funds, the amount a company is willing to pay to buy back one of its stock shares. The price difference between bid and ask is the commission. (See Ask Price.)

Blue Chip Stocks

Common stock in a nationally known company with good stability, i.e., with a proven ability to make money (profit) and pay dividends in good times and bad.

Bond

A certificate of debt issued by an organization. A bond's life spans 7 to 30 years. Bond owners receive a set amount of interest, payable every six months (semi-annually). Bond owners' claims against the company are senior to stock owners'. Bond Par/Face Value is the dollar amount printed on the bond certificate. The amount of interest paid is based on par value. For example, an 8% bond with a par value of $1,000, pays $80 per year (.08 × $1,000 = $80.) (See Municipal, Corporate, and Government Bonds.)

Bond Rating

A measure of the risk of various bonds. AAA is the safest, and D is the most risky.

Book Value

The value of everything a company owns minus what it owes. If the result is divided by the total number of stock shares, it is then known as book value per share.

Broker

Short for stockbroker. (See Stockbroker.)

Bull/Bull Market

Bull—A person who believes the stock market will rise. Bull Market—A rising market. Memory Aid—The horns of the bull point up. (See Bear/Bear Market.)

Call

When you buy a call, you buy the opportunity to purchase 100 shares of a particular stock at a given price by a given date. You are expecting the stock price to increase. Calls are handled by Option Exchanges similar to the NYSE and AMEX. Buying calls is risky; selling calls is conservative. (See Put.)

Callable Bond

A bond that can be redeemed or "called in" before maturity. In this event, bondholders would be paid a price (call price) higher than the face value of the bond.

Capital Gain/Loss

The profit/loss resulting from the sale of a capital asset. Capital Asset—Property (real estate, stocks, bonds, etc.) held for the purpose of bringing in profit. Note: "Capital gain/loss" is not related to the term "capital market."

Capital Market

A collective term that describes buy/sell action. The Capital Market includes long-term (more than one year) money tools such as stocks and bonds. (See Money Market.)

Cash Account

A common type of brokerage account in which the investor pays the full price for his purchases. (See Margin.)

Certificate

A document imprinted with information about the stock/ bond issue. Information may include serial number, transfer agent's name, par value, and a statement limiting the holder's financial liability to the company. Unless the certificate states "non-voting," the owner has voting rights.

Certificate of Deposit (CD)

This short-term money market tool is issued by banks in various denominations commonly starting at $2,500. Investors loan the face amount to the banks, and at maturity, the banks repay the face amount plus interest. Maturities range from one month to one year.

Certified Financial Planner

A title earned by someone who has passed five comprehensive exams. The exams include insurance, employee benefit and pension programs, taxes, and investments.

Closed-End Fund

A company with only a limited number of shares to sell. Share value is determined by supply and demand. (See Open-End Fund.)

Collateral Trust Bond

A bond which pledges other stocks and bonds as security for

its loan. The stocks and bonds must have a face value of at least 25% more than the face amount of the loan. (See Bond.)

Commerical Paper

This is a short-term (no more than 270 days) I.O.U. issued by a well-known company. Minimum purchase amount is $100,000. Commercial paper is usually bought by other corporations.

Commission(s)

Fees paid for services. For example, to stockbrokers for buying and/or selling stock.

Commodities

Highly risky investments in contracts for the future delivery of various agricultural and mineral products. Sometimes referred to as "futures contracts."

Common Stock

See Stock.

Confirmation

A memo sent to an investor by a brokerage firm. It contains all pertinent information about a buy or sale performed by the brokerage for the investor.

Consumers' Price Index (CPI)

A measurement of the price of a group of consumer goods. The measurement is compared with past prices to show any change and is expressed as a percentage.

Convertible/Convertibility

A provision of some bonds and preferred stock which allows the trade of the bond or stock for a set number of common stock shares of the issuing organization.

Convertible Bond

A bond that can be traded (converted) for company common stock. (See Bond.)

Corporate Bond

A bond issued by a company. This bond usually pays the highest rate of interest of any bond. For specific types see Debenture, Collateral Trust, Mortgage Bond, and Equipment Trust Certificate.

Coupon

A small certificate attached to a bond. The bondholder exchanges this certificate for an interest payment.

Coupon Bond

A bond which carries coupons which must be presented for interest payments. (See Bond.)

Coupon Rate

A general term for the interest percent payable on a bond. (See Bond.)

Cumulative Preferred

A stock with the provision that if one or more dividends are unpaid, the unpaid dividends must be settled before any dividends may be paid to common stockholders.

Debenture

The most common type of bond issued by a corporation. This type of bond is backed only by a company's "credit worthiness" and reputation. No real property is pledged. Subordinated Debenture—A debenture which receives payment only after the other existing bonds are paid. (See Bond.)

Discount

A price below face (par) value. (See also Premium.)

Discount Broker(age)

Fees (commissions) charged are less than those charged by full-service brokers. No research and/or advice is offered to investors. Buy/sell capabilities are the same as with full-service brokers.

Diversification

Spreading investments among various companies in different industries and/or using different types of money tools. This minimizes your risk.

Dividend

A payment to stockholders. The amount of the payment and the time it will be paid is decided by the company. Each shareholder receives so much per share. Dividends may be paid in cash or with additional shares of stock.

Dollar Cost Averaging

Purchasing a stock at regular intervals with a fixed amount of dollars, regardless of the current price of the stock. Your average cost per share will actually be lower than the average price per share for the period.

Dow Jones Industrial Average

An average of the market price of 30 different stocks. This is the most quoted of all averages. This and others are listed in Part Three of this book.

EE/E Bonds

See Government Saving Bonds.

Estate

All that you own. May be thought of as net worth.

Equipment Trust Certificate

A bond issued by transportation companies such as airlines and railroads. Company aircraft or railroad cars, etc. are used as security for the bonds. (See Bond.)

Exchange Privilege

The right to exchange shares of one mutual fund for those of another. Usually all funds involved are sold by the same company.

Ex-Dividend

Synonym for "without dividend." The buyer of a stock "ex-dividend" would *not* receive the dividend which had just been declared (announced.)

Face Value

See Par/Face Value.

FDIC (Federal Deposit Insurance Corporation)

See FSLIC.

FSLIC (Federal Savings and Loan Insurance Corporation)

Corporations that insure money deposited in banks, savings and loans, credit unions, and thrifts. Amounts are insured up to a $100,000 limit.

Financial Planner

A professional who has extensive knowledge about insurance, taxes, employee benefit and pension programs, and stock market investments. This person can fit all the pieces together for a personal financial plan.

Fixed Income Investment

An investment that pays a fixed, unchanging amount of interest or dividends.

Fundamental Approach

A method of analyzing investment possibilities. This method studies growth potential, profits, earnings, and management. (See Technical Approach.)

General Obligation Bond

The most common type of municipal bond. It is backed only by the faith, credit, and taxing power of the issuing local government.

Ginnie Mae (GNMA) Government National Mortgage Association

A government issue similar to housing authority bonds. Payment to holders comes from mortgage payments.

Going Public

When a company owned by just a few, often family or friends, decides to offer its stock for sale to the general public.

Government Savings Bonds (Series EE and HH)

Bonds sold by the U.S. Government. They are registered in the owner's name and are not transferable. These are the safest of all bonds. You may own Series E/H or may now purchase the new EE/HH. They are compared below:

Series E	Series EE	Series H/HH
You pay 75% of face value.	You Pay 50% of face value.	You trade E/EEs for face value.
Yield varies with time of purchase.	Yield now 7.5% min. but can be much higher.	Yield is 7.5% paid semi-annually.

(See Government Issues in Chapter 4.)

Growth Stock

Any of a group of stocks of companies growing faster than the general economy. These companies keep most of their earnings to enable further growth. These stocks usually pay low or no dividends.

HH/H Bonds

See Government Savings Bonds.

Income Stock

Stocks which pay stockholders a large portion, relative to other stocks, of the company's earnings.

Individual Retirement Account (IRA)

A tax-sheltered account set up by an individual. Amounts paid in may be subtracted from your gross income before taxes are figured.

Industrial Revenue Bond

A type of municipal bond. Bondholders receive payments from the rent received from those who use the factories or industrial parks built by the money obtained through bond sales.

Inflation

Constantly increasing prices.

Interest

The rent paid by borrowers to lenders for the use of money.

Invest/Investment

To commit money to some organization in hope of profit.

Investment Advisory Service

A company to which investors can subscribe that publishes periodic newsletters. These newsletters contain buy/sell advice and other information.

Investment Company

A corporation whose sole objective is the profitable reinvestment of its stockholders' monies in other companies' stocks and/or bonds.

Keogh

A tax-sheltered retirement plan used by self-employed. Money put in a Keogh account can be subtracted from current income before taxes are figured.

Liabilities

Everything a person or company owes. Its debts. (See Assets, Net Assets.)

Limited Partnership

A business arrangement that has many tax advantages. The name reflects the limited liability and limited management participation of the members (partners).

Liquidity

The ease of "cashing-in," or getting, your money from an investment.

Listed

Stock which you can trade that is registered on a national or regional stock exchange. (See Over-the-Counter.)

Living Trust

A group of orders that deals with an estate and that goes into effect during the life of the person who creates them and continues in effect after his death.

Load

The sales fee or commission of a mutual fund.

Long-Term Capital Gain/Loss

A profit or loss realized in an investment which lasted more than one year. Long-term gains receive highly favorable tax treatment.

Maintenance Call/Margin Call

A "call" or notice issued by a brokerage firm to investors who have bought "on margin." The brokerage requires that stock(s) used as collateral for these margin loans maintain a minimum value. If the stock's value falls below this minimum, the maintenance call is issued, and investors must provide additional money to the margin account or sell the stock and take the loss. (See Margin, Margin Account.)

Margin

When you buy stock "on margin," you borrow part of the purchase price from the stock brokerage firm. The brokerage supplies the extra "margin" of money needed for the purchase. You must be prepared to meet maintenance calls. (See Maintenance Call/Margin Call.)

Margin Account

You and your broker may set up this type of account for buying stocks/bonds "on margin." (See Margin.)

Market Order

An order by a customer to a broker to buy or sell at the best price available, i.e., there is no set buy or sell price.

Market Price/Value

The last reported price at which an issue sells. Bonds—The price received by a bondholder if the bond is sold before maturity. Bond market values change in the opposite direction of market place interest rates. Market interest rate rises will decrease bond market values.

Maturity

A date, printed on a debt certificate (bond, CD, etc.), showing when the money loaned will be repaid to investors. The amount repaid will be the par value or face value of the certificate.

Money

A storage of value. Money serves three purposes: (1) It is widely accepted in exchange for goods and services. (2) It is a yardstick by which the value of other things is measured. (3) It is a convenient method of storing or saving purchasing power or value.

Money Market

A collective term that describes buy/sell action. The Money Market includes short-term (less than one year) money tools such at T-Bills and CDs. (See Capital Market.)

Money Market Funds

Mutual funds which invest solely in short-term debt issues such as T-Bills and Bankers' Acceptances. Investments can be withdrawn easily and these funds are generally safe.

Money Market Savings Account

A bank savings account that pays interest at rates based on Money Market rates. (See Money Market.)

Mortgage Bond

A bond secured by property. (See Bond.)

Municipal Bond

Any of a variety of bonds issued by local governmental units such as states, counties, cities, and school districts. The interest is not federally taxed and may avoid some state and local taxes. For individual types see Industrial Revenue Bond, Revenue Bond, General Obligation Bond, and Special Assessment Bond.

Municipal Notes

Loans by investors to municipalities (states, cities, school districts) and backed by sums these government units expect to receive. The source of anticipated money is indicated by the name of the note. Typical maturities range from one to five years.

Municipal Note Names
TANs = Tax Anticipation Notes
RANs = Revenue Anticipation Notes
BANs = Bank Anticipation Notes

Mutual Fund

The pooling of investment money into a fund managed by professionals. The purpose of the fund is to make profits for the investors.

Net Assets

The resulting total when liabilities are subtracted from assets. The same as Net Worth. (See Assets, Liabilities.)

Net Asset Value (NAV)

The total value of all debt-free property owned by a mutual fund (the book value). To state as a per share figure, simply divide NAV by total shares.

Net Worth

See Net Assets.

New York Stock Exchange (NYSE)

The largest organization functioning as a clearing house for the nation-wide buying and selling of stocks and bonds.

No-Load Fund

A mutual fund that does not charge a sales fee or commission.

Note

A promise to pay back a medium-term (one to ten years) loan.

Now Accounts

A bank account where amounts are withdrawn from a savings account to cover checks. Interest-bearing checking accounts operate this way. NOW is short for Negotiated Order of Withdrawal.

Odd Lot

An amount of stock less than a 100-share unit. (See Round Lot.)

Offer Price

The amount an investor would have to pay for a share of a mutual fund.

Open-End Fund

An investment company (mutual fund) that has no fixed amount of shares it can offer for sale. The more buyers it has, the more shares it will offer. The company will buy back shares at any time. (See Closed-End Fund, Mutual Fund.)

Option

The right to buy or sell a specific stock at a set price within a stated time.

Over-The-Counter (OTC)

Stocks which you can trade that are not listed on a national or regional exchange. (See Listed.)

Paper Loss

A loss which you have not yet claimed on a stock or bond you still hold. If 100 shares of stock go down three points and you have not yet sold them, you have a paper loss of $300. (See Paper Profit.)

Paper Profit

A gain which you have not claimed on a stock or bond you still hold. If 100 shares of stock go up three points and you have not yet sold, you have a paper profit of $300. (See Paper Loss.)

Par/Face Value

A dollar amount (price) stated on the certificate of stocks, bonds, etc. by the issuing company. Do not confuse with market value. Par values do not change; market values do.

With Stock—A dollar amount assigned to stock by the issuing company.

With Common Stock—This value is meaningless.

With Preferred Stock—The par value is the basis upon which the dividend is figured. For example, an 8% preferred with a par value of $100 will pay $8 a year (.08 × $100 = $8.) (See Bond, Stock.)

Penalty

The fine some banks impose if your balance drops below a certain minimum. With CDs—The fine imposed if you withdraw your money before the assigned date (maturity). Fines may be in the form of additional costs to you or in the loss of interest payments.

Penny Stock

Slang for stocks selling at very low prices, usually less than $3 per share.

Point

With stock, each point equals $1. If a stock's value goes up 3 points, it actually goes up $3.

Portfolio

The collection of stocks, bonds, mutual fund shares and the like which are owned by an individual or institution.

Pre-Emptive Right

The right of every common stockholder to maintain his proportionate share of ownership in a company. This right gives present owners first chance at newly offered stock.

Preferred Stock

See Stock.

Premium

Bonds which are selling at a premium have a price above their face (par) value. (See also Discount.)

Primary Issue

The first offering of a batch of stock by a company. These are shares not sold before. (See Secondary Market/Offering.)

Prime Rate

The interest rate charged by banks for short-term loans. This rate is only offered to the bank's best customers.

Principal

The original amount of money committed to an investment.

Progressive Income Tax

A tax based on the amount of income you earn. As you earn more, you pay a higher percentage of your earnings to taxes.

Proxy Statement

A legal document which when signed, transfers voting rights to another person.

Put

A contract giving the right to sell a specific stock at a set price within a set time. The buyer of a put expects the price to fall. (See Call.)

Quote

The reporting of a price.

Redeem

When a *company* redeems a bond, it pays back the bondholder's loaned money plus any interest. When a *person* redeems a bond, he receives back his loaned money plus any interest.

Registered Bond

A bond issued to an individual whose name is recorded in the files of the issuing company. (See Bond, Bearer Bond.)

Registered Representative

A title for a broker. (See Stockbroker.)

Return

The profits on investments. Includes more than a yield, i.e., it includes dividends, interest, capital gains, etc. (See Yield.)

Revenue Bond/Housing Authority Bond

A type of municipal bond. Payments to bondholders come from fees (rents, fares) paid by users of the project built by the bond money. Revenue bonds are used by airports, rapid transit systems, college dorms, public housing, etc.

Rights

A certificate giving the opportunity to buy a set number of shares of a specific stock at a price below market value. The certificate usually expires within four weeks. (See Warrant.)

Risk

The chance of loss.

Round Lot

A 100-share unit of stock. (See Odd Lot.)

Roll-Over

The transfer of money from one tax-deferred account to another. Often, this can be accomplished without tax consequences.

Secondary Market/Offering

This refers to the usual buying and selling among stock/bond owners and other investors. The company that first issues the stock/bond does not participate. The shares being traded were originally bought from the company, but in the secondary offerings, trading is just among investors.

Securities

A general term used to describe any stock, bond, note, bill, etc. One of the most over-used terms in the world of money. There are two broad classifications of securities outlined below:

Fixed-Income Securities—Payment of a specific amount at a specific time. Payments do not change.

Variable-Income Securities—Payments not specified. Payments vary according to the fortunes of the issuing company.

Serial/Series/Term Bonds

Bonds may be sold with different maturity dates or with different dates of issue. The table below shows their differences:

Serial Bonds— *usually municipals*— Same issue date, different maturity dates.

| Series Bonds— *infrequent*— | Different issue dates, same maturity date. |
| Term Bonds— *corporate*— | Same issue and maturity dates. |

Shares

Units of ownership of a corporation.

Short-Term Capital Gain/Loss

A profit or loss realized in less than one year. Tax treatment is as ordinary income. (See Long-Term Capital Gain/Loss, Capital Gain/Loss.)

SIPC (Securities Investor Protection Corporation)

An insurance company that protects investors from brokerage house bankruptcy losses. Maximum amount protected is $100,000.

Special Assessment Bond

A type of municipal bond. Bondholders receive payments from taxes assessed against the users of the project built by the bond money. Users include water or sewer works, streets, etc.

Speculation

Accepting higher risks in anticipation of higher gains.

Split

To divide shares of stock. A company which declares a two-for-one split would double the number of shares. Each share would then be worth half the previous price.

Stock

The transferable certificates that show ownership in a company.

Common Stock—The most usual class of stock issued by a company. It qualifies the investor for voting privileges and dividends, if any.

Preferred Stock—A class of stock which has a claim on company earnings (dividends) which must be satisified before any payments may be made to common stockholders. It has priority over common stock if the company is liquidated.

Stock Market

The collective term which includes all the organizations engaged in buying and selling stocks, bonds, etc.

Stock Power

A legal form that will, when signed by the owner and attached to a stock certificate, authorize the transfer (sale) of the stock share. This legal form is used by an owner who keeps his own certificates. It is used when the certificate itself can not be signed, for example, if the owner is traveling.

Street Name Account

When this account type is used, stocks and bonds are left with the brokerage firm and registered in the firm's name. This eliminates the investor's handling of the stocks and bonds for all buy/sell actions. Investors receive statements indicating they are the owner of record.

Stockbroker

Also called Account Executive, Registered Representative, or Broker. A licensed agent who negotiates the public's orders to buy and sell various money tools (stocks, bonds, mutual fund shares, etc.).

Super Now Account

A bank checking account that pays interest at rates based on Money Market rates. (See NOW Account, Money Market.)

Tax Avoidance

Any legal method of sheltering income from taxation.

Tax-Deferred

An investment designed to delay the payment of taxes.

Tax Evasion

Any illegal method of attempting to keep from paying taxes.

Tax-Free

Income from investments that is exempt from taxation.

Tax Shelter

An investment designed to avoid or delay the payment of taxes.

Technical Approach

A method of analyzing investment possibilities. This method studies the history, price movements, and patterns of an investment. Those using this method keep many graphs and charts, hence their nickname "chartists." (See Fundamental Approach.)

Term Bond

See Serial/Series/Term Bonds.

Testamentary Trust

See Will.

Treasury Issues

There are three types of these government issues:

Treasury Bills (T-Bills)—*Short Term (3 mo.–1 yr.)* — $1,000 Minimum. When you buy, you will pay less than face value, similar to savings bonds.

Treasury Notes—*Medium Term (1 yr.–10 yr.)*—$10,000 Minimum. When you buy, you pay face value.

Treasury Bonds—*Long Term (5 yr.–30 yr.)*—$1,000 Minimum. When you buy, you pay face value.

Warrant

A certificate giving the opportunity to buy a set number of shares of a specific stock at a price below market value. The certificate usually expires within five years. (See Rights.)

Wealth

Enough money to satisfy all present and future wants and needs.

Will

A legal document prepared by a person before death which states how he wishes his possessions to be disposed of after his death. Wills should be drawn up with the assistance of an attorney. The legal name for a will is testamentary trust.

Yield

The dividend or interest paid on your investment. It is expressed as a percentage of the current price of the investment. (See Return.)

INDEX

Also consult the Table of Contents and Part Four's Dictionary.

167

168 *MAKE MONEY MAKE MONEY*